100 Million Dollar Selling

The handbook for sales
professionals who want to win

By
Ferdinand Roberts

Version. 2.0
August 2017

First published in 2017

ISBN: 9781521957936

Imprint: Independently published

Table of Contents

Preface

This book has been a number of years in the making, and I'm happy that it's finally at a stage where I can share it with you.

In the last 24 years, I have sold more than $100m worth of software globally. I'm sure I would have sold a great deal more if I'd known in the early days of my sales career what I know now. I decided to write this book to share with you the lessons I've learned so that you can succeed in your chosen sales career and create options for yourself that most people only dream about.

I've written the kind of book that I like to read. One that is practical, based on experience and can be consumed quickly – on a flight, or read over a day or two.

If you need a quick guide to negotiation, or are about to embark on a lead generation exercise you have a chapter that you can read quickly to equip yourself with the details of what's really important.

I've tried wherever possible to provide examples, to put into context a background to some of my thoughts, but also to provide insight into my beliefs when it comes to sales.

The ability to sell has been a great asset to me throughout life. It has given me purpose and taught me valuable lessons. I've lost deals that I've learned from and I've won deals that have propelled me forward. On one level, sales is very simple. You get out of it what you put in.

When you look at the basic role of a salesperson, it's to motivate another person to firstly, buy into you as a person, then the company you represent, and finally the product or service you are offering.

It's a profession full of responsibility and one that I believe takes passion to be great at. The greatest salespeople are, in my experience, always passionate; although they may show it in different ways.

It's not always the gregarious, golfing, corporate-entertaining salesperson who wins the deal. Passion can be displayed in the pride they take in the work that they do. It can be seen in the quality of the materials they give a prospective customer. It can be seen in the command they have of the numbers associated with a deal. It is obvious in the diligence they show when working to uncover the pain points that a customer has.

Whether you are completely new to sales or are reading this because you want to take your business or career to the next level, my hope is that you benefit greatly from this book. I have a love for sales because the act of selling has created options for me and given me a lifestyle that would have been very difficult to achieve in a standard 9 to 5 role.

If I were to summarize in a few sentences what I've learned from all of my years selling it would be this.

- Be prepared for hard work, embrace it.

- Think about the problems of your target customer, the key to your value proposition lies there.

- Have a genuine love for what you do and the product you sell – it will make your job a great deal more enjoyable and that will show in the results you achieve.

- Surround yourself with capable, competent people. Selling is a team effort.

If you really care about selling, about providing for yourself and your family, about the benefit of what you are doing for your customers and clients, sales will be a profession from which you can benefit greatly.

I have, and I am proud to be able to share with you what I've learned.

Ferdi
August 2017.

Chapter 1: The basics of selling

In this book, we are going to break down the key elements of selling and look at each forensically so that you can understand what you need to do to sell more effectively.

You may be starting a new business or have a great idea that you'd like to pursue, but for some reason you just can't 'sell it'

You may find that people who are less experienced than you, maybe even less capable than you, are progressing in their career because they 'sell' themselves more effectively.

There may be lots of reasons why you are interested in selling, but for this book to be effective you need to take the core tenets of what I am about to share with you and make them part of your everyday business practice. It's the consistency with which you execute the tactics and strategy outlined in this book that will determine your success. That, and good old-fashioned hard work.

You get out – what you put in

When I was in my early 20's I was working for a company called Aspect Communications. It was a great company with a great product. I worked with wonderful, talented people and they had an enviable reputation.

What they didn't have was a particularly big presence in the financial services sector. They had a few U.S. examples but mostly customers came from the outsourcing sector, the telesales and customer care departments of retailers, and a growing presence in the mobile communications and travel sector.

I joined to take responsibility for growing the UK financial services sector for them.

I joined the company at 22 and was completely obsessed with making a success of my new position. I relished the opportunity to grow a new market sector for the company. Knowing little about the market at that time, I consumed as much information as I could, reading articles about the sector, going to seminars and trade events to educate myself.

When faced with the challenge of getting meetings with target customers (the main banks and insurance companies of the UK), I would ask their PA's for the fax number for my target customer and sent a weekly 'round-up' of interesting news stories from the industry, together with some cartoons such as Dilbert to help lighten the reading a little.

I should say this was in the early 90's, so the concept of sending an email or using some marketing software to do this was still not available at scale. My weekly 1-2 page fax was my way of keeping in contact with my target audience. My name and contact details were at the end of each page and of course on the cover page of the fax. Think of this as a pre-cursor to a 'share' on LinkedIn.

I chose articles that were self-serving of course, such as how improved customer care could add millions to your bottom line, or stories about how competitor 'A' had recently revamped their call centre and were achieving results of 'X' millions in savings or increased revenue.

My choice of articles was partly dependent on the content available that week but equally dependent on initiatives that I knew were important for my target customers.

As most of my target clients were public companies they are required to publish annual financials that were typically accompanied by statements from the chairman and the various heads of division such as sales, IT etc.

These statements were a perfect source for understanding what was important to them as a company and how strategically significant each initiative was.

When sending my fax to each contact I would handwrite a note referring back to an initiative that they had mentioned in one of these statements and refer them to something that we had announced or perhaps a competitive bank had announced. Where appropriate, I would then suggest that it might be useful for us to meet and discuss how we believed we could help.

It personalized the communication, but also showed that I was taking the time to understand the market, and more importantly, the specific challenges faced by my target company.

When I got a response, and trust me, that simple weekly fax was one of the most effective tools I had in my early days of developing the UK financial services sector for Aspect, I made the most of it. I made sure I got as much information as I possibly could about the challenges they faced, what technology they were using, what they liked about the partners they worked with, etc. I'll be covering the process of 'needs discovery' in an upcoming chapter but this is one of the most important phases in the sales process.

Now, while I wouldn't suggest faxing as the most effective means of communicating with target clients today, what I am advocating is putting the legwork into understanding the challenges of your target customer and asking the right questions. This is how you gain maximum insights into the customers' needs as a means of developing a proper value proposition. This means that when you do connect with your target market, you've got something they will want to hear. This, of course is a fundamental component of selling.

Before we wrap up this chapter and start to look at the individual components of selling, let's summarize. Selling is the process of engaging, listening, demonstrating you understand and providing 'value and insight' that your target customer appreciates and benefits from.

It means recognizing that unless you are lucky enough to work for a company that has a market monopoly you are in a competitive environment, and if you aren't paying attention to what your customer wants, your competitor is, and you will lose.

Conversely, if you have a thorough understanding of your market, your products, the needs of the customer, how you can help, what makes you the obvious choice and what the steps are to get to yes, you will be successful.

Okay, let's dive into the detail of selling.

Chapter 2: Know your customer

Consider this the first question you should ask yourself before you start: Who is my customer?. It's important for lots of reasons but not the least of which is that it allows you to make the maximum use of your time and resources when engaging in a sales process. It's the planning you put into the sales journey, before you take a single step.

To understand who your customer is, there are some fundamental questions that you should answer. Here are some of the most important:

What type of company buys the type of product or service that I sell?

This sounds pretty obvious but knowing who buys your type of product or service allows you to look at their characteristics. You should note the size of company (number of employees), the turnover of the company (are they a small or large business in terms of revenue?), the geographic spread and location of the customer (are they multi-site or international in terms of geographic spread?).

All of these insights, and more, allow you start to create a photo-fit of the type of customer that is buying your products. Armed with that you can start to look at customers who match that profile.

What problems does my product or service solve?

A product or service that succeeds is one that ultimately solves a problem for people. Unfortunately, the world is full of products and services looking for a problem to solve.

You must first understand the problem before you can appreciate how your product or service solves it for the customer. A great way to familiarize yourself with the answers to this question is to spend time with your existing customers. They will gladly share with you what issues they faced and how your product or service helped them to solve it.

By understanding how you've helped your existing customers you can more readily identify these challenges in other businesses. This allows you to articulate the benefits to a potential prospect. This is also valuable when presenting to prospects in a formal manner as it allows you to illustrate benefits by way of real-world examples. This is always a far more powerful means of getting your message across and engaging your audience.

Do I have multiple 'buyer personas' that I am serving?

A 'buyer persona' is simply a grouping of customers that share common characteristics. This is a great question to ask if you have a product or service that can be easily adapted to meet the needs of multiple target markets.

For example, if your company has developed a great note-taking application, you may appeal to:

- students who need it for class-notes
- for journalists for press briefings or interviews
- for start-ups who want to collaborate and share ideas
- for corporates who want to foster interdepartmental communication

The list goes on. You should create a list of personas that your product appeals to as a means of building your go-to-market plan.

You can then start to think about how best to engage each persona, i.e. the channels, the messaging etc.

Where does the problem that you solve exist in your target company?

By understanding the nature of the pain points that exist within a business you can start to understand who is affected by these challenges. This will also highlight who is most likely to be impacted by their improvement. They may not be the most influential in the decision making process but you definitely need to know who they are so you can sense-check your understanding of the issues they face. They are often the 'coaches' in an account, i.e. they will help you to navigate the decision-making process in larger organizations and provide guidance on the priority of the issues faced by their business.

What role in your target business has been most instrumental in winning previous deals (technical, operational, CXO)?

This will help you identify the key roles that you must engage with as you build your value proposition. For example, if your company helps to improve the effectiveness of marketing spend, you certainly need to engage with the executive responsible for marketing. You may also need to engage with the head of sales, the technology team (as the software needs to 'play nice' with every other software application that they are using today). You get the idea.

For which markets do I have the most competitive advantage?

This question is particularly worth asking in markets that are highly commoditized. In other words, the product and pricing differentiation may not be that significant. It is worthwhile therefore for you to understand if there are other points of differentiation that you can leverage.

If you've got strengths in a particular vertical market for example, you should continue to press that as much as you can. Beyond that, you should look at the next obvious adjacent market as a venn diagram of needs will probably show a fair degree of overlap. Of course this principle is valid even for niche markets.

If you ask yourself these questions, you will start to build up a picture of likely candidates for inclusion in your target market. You should view this as the master list.

You then need to start to segment your master list into cohort groups which can be further prioritized. For example, if you have identified that the pharmaceutical market is a good fit for your product, there are small, medium and large pharma companies that you could target. Which is best suited? You should prioritize based on 'best fit'.

Segmenting further you may look at geographies to identify where best to apply the limited resources and time that you have. You should prioritize the geographies accordingly.

You may then wish to apply a further filter that looks at the competitive landscape. Unless you are lucky enough to sell in a monopolistic market you will have competitors who have already closed some business in your target market. By overlaying the competitive landscape against your target list you will be able to further prioritize where you spend your time.

What you should end up with after this exercise is a number of segments based on size, location, competitive landscape etc. and from this you should prioritize your market engagement. Note, you may have further filters that you need to apply for your given market but the principle of 'focus' is what's important here.

Personally I have a preference for going after the biggest fish first. It's hard to land them, but when you do, the smaller players in that market are far easier to sell to. It's also often just as much effort to sell to a small business as it can be to a large corporate, so for improved 'return on time invested' I've found the larger the deal you can work on, the better.

That's a broad statement but one I've found holds true over the years.

Chapter 3: Lead generation

The lifeblood of all sales organizations is its leads. Without a constant stream of leads your sales engine runs out of fuel and everything comes to a grinding halt. If you've worked in sales for a reasonable period of time you may be familiar with the boom and bust cycle. This is typical in an organization that relies on its salespeople to generate leads, **and** move newly qualified leads through a sales process. What I've seen happen typically follows this pattern:

- Salesperson makes a substantial number of outbound calls and stimulates some interest.
- Salesperson follows up on this interest and starts to move the prospects through the sales pipeline.
- Salesperson spends more and more of their time engaged in the sales cycles of the newly created pipeline.
- Salesperson sticks with these deals until closure.
- Salesperson starts hitting the phones again to generate new leads.

On the face of it, this may seem fine; however this leads to a roller-coaster pipeline. When the salesperson is prospecting, the pipeline is filling and when they are moving them through the sales process, the old leads are not being replaced with new ones. This is a dangerous cycle that, depending on when the ups and downs come, can make or break your year. This is not an advisable approach to building your pipeline.

A more sustainable and predictable approach that I have found useful is dedicating a fixed amount of time to prospecting each week, or, depending on your industry and the visibility you have on your closure rate, working until you have generated X number of qualified leads. Either approach may work for you but the principle is the same in both cases.

You should be working to ensure that you always have deals in the pipeline that you can work on, and you are not spending large periods of the year where your pipeline visibility is opaque. Being disciplined about this is one of the most important things you can do as a sales professional.

The essentials of lead generation:

There's a saying *'The customers you have are the customers you want'*

This means that the characteristics of your best customers are the characteristics to look for in prospective customers. If you sell product A and your existing customers have the following characteristics:

- Medium sized businesses
- Manufacturing focus
- 100+ employees
- Revenue of $10m +
- U.S. based

What does this tell you? It tells you that a good place to start looking for prospects are manufacturing companies in the U.S. that meet that exact criteria. Sounds simple, right?. You might think so but I'm amazed at how often I've seen this basic rule ignored as companies inherently feel like they need to be looking elsewhere when sales stall. Never ignore your core market. It's fine to start looking at adjacent markets over time, but not at the expense of the customer-types who currently pay the bills.

Laser focus – versus – 'Spray and pray' lead generation.

'Spray and pray' is an expression used to describe sales campaigns that are based on luck rather than judgement.

It's based on the simple premise that the more people or companies that you reach out to, the greater the pipeline you'll create, right? Wrong.

The 'spray' involves activities such as mass emailing and the 'pray' describes what you're doing while you wait in hope that one of those emails may encourage a prospect to respond and reach out to you.

Email campaigns are fine, but start by making sure that the profile of companies or individuals in your email campaign match the criteria of your target market. We're looking for quality rather than quantity.

Laser focus, as the name suggests involves being ultra-specific about the type of prospect you are trying to engage. As with any marketing campaign, it subscribes to the adage, 'garbage in, garbage out', so make sure that if you are planning a campaign that the data that you use is current and accurate.

As an indication, for 1000 records, you should expect that 10-20% of your email or telephone records for your contacts become obsolete every 6 months (depending on the market you operate in). If you've got a two-year-old list, almost 40% of that list could be completely out of date.

Lead generation is a continuous process

As mentioned at the outset, you should view lead generation as the lifeblood of your company. Without leads you don't have the fuel you need to drive your business forward.

Like any machine, if you cut off the fuel, or the fuel is intermittent, the efficiency of your company and its ability to move forward will be negatively impacted.

You must have a solid focus on lead generation at all times. Avoid the feast and famine approach that many salespeople find themselves slipping into. It's easy when you are busy, to forget that after the current deal you are working on is closed, you will need another deal to close, and another.

Think about it in these terms. If it takes you an average of two months to close a deal, you might think that six deals a year is a good year, and perhaps it is. If you've got continuous lead generation in place however, what's to stop you closing 12 deals a year, or 24, or one every week?

The best salespeople I've seen and worked with have a continuous pipeline and therefore, can continuously close deals.

You've heard the expression that 'success breeds success'. You may also have witnessed this in the form of a salesperson who seems to be on a streak. They close a big deal and soon another big deal, and another. There's a simple explanation for this – when you experience success in sales you feel you've 'cracked the code' and your confidence level increases.

This increased confidence can also be seen by prospective customers – they see the confidence with which you are presenting your product or service, the confidence you have in your voice, your stance – the whole nine yards. These are some of the subtleties of selling that prospects pick up on that can make all the difference. Once you start to succeed, you'll be in this 'zone' and the only way to remain there is to continue winning business. The best salespeople figure this out quickly and do all that they can to stay there.

What's the secret? The secret is to not lose sight of what got you that last win. It's doing everything I subscribe to in this book, consistently and diligently.

Chapter 4: Getting to no - The importance of qualifying out.

Have you ever received a call from a prospective customer out of the blue wanting to meet you as soon as possible to discuss what you can do for them? It happens, right? Every salesperson has had this happen at some point. When it first happens you can't believe your luck.

There you were, developing your complex market engagement strategy when all of a sudden, opportunity presents itself. It would be rude not to get a date in the calendar immediately, strike while the iron is hot – wouldn't it? Not so fast. Just ask yourself:

- Why is there sudden urgency?
- Who is asking to meet with you?
- What is their role?
- Why are they asking to meet?
- What's the compelling event?
- How did they come across your company?
- Is there an active project?
- Are they a decision maker?

These are basic qualification questions. You have no way of knowing whether this is an opportunity until you exercise the discipline of asking qualifying questions. It's tempting for sure to convince yourself that the caller must be interested if they went to the trouble of seeking you out and calling you to set up a meeting. They may be interested, but you have to view this inbound interest with a degree of professional skepticism. Let me explain why.

I've had success in sales over long periods of time for many reasons but one of the most important is my proactivity. What I mean is, I proactively engage my market. I do my research, I pick up the phone, I network, I ask questions.

I keep in contact and I ensure that at the moment of truth, when an opportunity presents itself in that clients' business, I am there, or I am the first person they call. I do not leave it to chance. I do not wait for the phone to ring, I am there, as ever-present as it's possible to be without becoming a source of annoyance.

You have got to assume that someone like me is selling against you in every single sales opportunity.

You have to assume that there is a hungry, persistent individual that has done the groundwork and is seeking to take from you, a deal that you may feel is rightfully yours.

I am saying this to illustrate a point. Let's take a look at that unexpected incoming phone call again. If you haven't spoken with this person before, the chances are, a salesperson more proactive than you has.

If you are agreeing to meet before you have a basic understanding of the challenges they have, you are going to a meeting unprepared, unsure if the person you are meeting is actually material to the decision making process.

The proactive sales person is equipped with this knowledge and may not be meeting the person you are meeting, but rather is meeting their boss, because they actually make the decision.

You may think, as you wait in reception that you are there to progress a sales opportunity, when in reality you are little more than what I like to call a 'professional visitor'.

For clarity, a professional visitor is a salesperson who understands so little about the selling process that they drift from meeting to meeting watching things happen to them rather than making things happen for them.

They 'show up and throw-up' to coin an often-used expression in the sales world. If you do this, you are not selling, you are professionally visiting.

They are the also-rans of the sales world, don't be one of them. Not only will your sales career be a short one, but you will have missed an opportunity to provide for yourself and your family in a way that most people never get the opportunity to do.

A more appropriate way to assess opportunities that has worked well for me is the concept of 'getting to no'. Let me explain.

If you examine the habits of successful sales people you will see that they are discerning in terms of how they spend their time. They ask questions to ensure a deal is real before spending time on it. This is an important habit to develop as it means you are not spending valuable time pursuing a deal that is not going to happen, at the expense of one that is. This sounds simple but practicing active qualification is something that does not come naturally to a lot of people.

The natural tendency is to engage in a sales cycle as long as it looks like there is a sale to be had. The challenge here is to determine if in fact there is a real deal in process. There are lots of non-deal related reasons why people may reach out to you.

Here are just a few:

- They are doing some market research in case they ever need to engage
- It's an area of personal interest to them so they wanted to know more
- Their boss asked them to see who was doing what in the market

- They work in the sector and need to keep abreast of what the market has to offer
- They are trying to get some competitive intelligence because they are friendly with someone who works with your competition
- They are writing a blog article and would like to know more

This list goes on, and in most cases the person reaching out may be quite happy to have you 'professionally visit' with them while your successful counterpart at your competitor is progressing an actual deal.

To avoid this situation, here are some questions that you should be asking to qualify every deal, and to gain some insight into whether there is a deal to be had, and if so what the process looks like to getting that deal done:

- How did you hear about us?
- Do you have a live project?
- Is this a budgeted initiative?
- Who will make the decision (financially, technologically)?
- What are your timeframes for a decision?
- Who is sponsoring this project?
- What happens if you do nothing, i.e. is there a compelling reason to do something?
- Who else are you talking to?
- What are the burning issues you are trying to address with this?
- Are there any competing projects that may impact your ability to progress with this one?

Asking some basic questions will allow you to determine how serious the enquiry is, and whether or not the company in question is in a serious buying process.

The degree to which they are able to answer these questions is a good reflection of where they are in their process. If they are well prepared you will receive well prepared answers. If there are large gaps and opaque responses, you can be pretty sure its reflective of how prepared they are to get engaged in the process.

This in itself does not mean that you should not engage with that prospect, it simply means that you need to understand from whom you can get the answers you need before engaging heavily with your time, and the resources of your company, to help this person.

It may seem like a pretty binary assessment, but sales is binary at its heart. You either win or you lose. There either is a deal or there isn't. You are either investing your time and getting a return or you are losing it.

The challenge with the last point is that you aren't just losing the non-deal that you are engaged in, you are most likely losing the actual deal that you could have been working on.

You have to be discerning with your time in sales because whether you have a daily, weekly, monthly, quarterly or yearly target to meet, the clock is ticking.

Each day spent on something that is non-productive is a day lost that you cannot recoup. You need to get to 'No' quickly, if that is the reality of the situation, so that you can make an investment in something that is going to provide a return on that time.
In sales it makes the difference between having a successful career and a job that you love, versus having no job. In that sense it is completely binary.

If you keep this reality at the forefront of your mind as you engage, or are engaged by potential clients, you are off to a great start. It doesn't mean you will be a great salesperson, but a well-qualified deal in which you have a good handle on the evaluation process and the pain points is a great place to start.

Bottom line: You need to evaluate each deal like your livelihood depends on it – because it does.

Chapter 5: The sales process.

Whenever we engage in buying something significant as a consumer, there is usually a well-defined process that we follow. If we are buying a house for the first time it can seem daunting. How do I get approved for a mortgage? How do I get the house valued? How do I insure the house? etc.

The process for the uninitiated can seem very complex. When we investigate further, we discover that although there are lots of moving parts to the purchase, there is in fact a well-defined series of steps to closure. If we follow these steps it will lead to us purchasing our home and overcoming what at first seemed like a gargantuan series of tasks.

Our bank or broker normally smoothes the way for us. They provide guidance on the process, they outline the steps, they provide quick and easy solutions to the peripheral requirements such as life assurance and home insurance. In doing so, they make life easier for us.

They break the process down into a series of steps, ensuring that they hand-hold us through the process. It should be noted that in return for simplifying and supporting us through this process, they not only secure our mortgage business, often they also secure our insurance and assurance business too.

As sales professionals, we too need a sales process. We should be able to clearly articulate to a potential buyer what that process looks like and provide a benefit to the user in following that process.

If we can achieve that, we have shifted the control of the process from the buyer, to ourselves as the seller and this is a subtle but very powerful shift that you must strive to achieve in every opportunity that you engage in. I'll explain why.

If you are engaging with a potential customer for the first time, they by definition have never done business with you before, or purchased your product or service before.

This means that you know best how your product or service can be bought and by defining this for a prospective client, you can gain control over the sales process and lead the prospect from step 1 to step 10 in a controlled and predictable manner.

As an example, when I was managing the sales organization for an e-procurement software business in Europe in the early 2000's, procurement departments had not purchased cloud-based procurement technologies in the past and as such we could define what the process looked like.

I knew that in order to convince these organizations to work with us we needed to provide them with a robust evaluation process and hands-on experience before they could make an informed decision. Armed with this, we developed an engaging educational, informational, instructional and experiential pre-sales process which sought to achieve the following:

Educational: We held regular educational sessions for procurement professionals that wanted to know more about the emerging e-procurement space. We engaged subject matter experts and existing customers to 'educate' the audience on the concepts of e-procurement. The important thing to note is that this was not a sales pitch. This was designed simply to explain the principles of e-procurement which involved everything from online tendering to e-auctions and beyond. Providing a grounding in the principles meant that this audience would have a base of knowledge on which we could build for the next phase.

Informational: Having equipped our target audience with a base understanding of the trends in the industry, we then sought to provide them with some informational insights regarding the benefits of e-procurement technologies. We did this by way of case studies and success stories from our existing customer base.

Utilizing the information we had garnered from our most successful implementations, we used informational sessions to equip the procurement professionals with the facts they needed to start to build the case for eProcurement in their own company.

Instructional: Armed with some case study materials and a good understanding of the benefits of eProcurement we then focused on actively demonstrating the concepts we had discussed to the target audience. In some cases, this was achieved through webinars (online seminars), or group sessions that we held every month.

The purpose of this was to provide generic high-level demonstrations that typically allowed the audience to gain a greater appreciation for the day to day application of this technology to their work. The sessions were designed to encourage participants to talk about the daily challenges of their job, which at that time was largely manual in nature. These discussions gave us the insights we needed to make the final sessions as valuable as possible.

Experiential: With the insights gained in the previous sessions we were able to ensure that the final session covered all of the challenges that we had discussed. The sessions were interactive in nature, with participants encouraged to get hands-on with the software, tackling the issues they faced in their day to day role.

This experience-based session was always my favorite as it gave my team and I an opportunity to see the participants experience what was for many of them, a step change in the way they carried out their work.

This 4 stage process was the initial pre-sales engagement closely followed by a prospect-specific review of their procurement practices, followed by a report on our findings.

Naturally, we made recommendations on improvements that we felt we could bring to their organization, together with a financial proposal outlining the investment required to deploy our solutions in their business.

Our close-rate was over 70% for anyone who went through the entire four-stage process with us. Equally, over time we came to recognize when people started to drop out of the process, what our pipeline stages were and how best to predict the close-rate for deals that were 'in process'.

The key takeaway from the example above is that when your buyer has not bought from you before, you are in the position to dictate the process that they must go through when evaluating or buying your product or service.

Not every buyer will want to stick rigidly to your process, but having one that you can encourage them to participate in is an absolute must. If you do not have one today, stop what you are doing and create one. It will have a transformative effect on your business.

The other primary benefit of having a sales process is that you get to measure progression and drop-off at each stage. This is important if you want to be able to predict and forecast more accurately your revenue over time.

The simplest way to explain this is as follows. Let's assume you have a 4 stage sales process.

Stage 1 is information gathering and information exchange, i.e. You speak with a prospect and gather information from them, which in turn allows you to share some information with them regarding your product. Let's assume for simplicity that 100% of the prospects that you speak with have this 2-way conversation with you. In other words 100% of your engaged market participates in this initial stage of your sales process.

Stage 2 is a more detailed information gathering exercise on your part, where you seek to understand more about your prospects business. You take the time to understand their challenges and the nuances of their business. The purpose of this stage is to enable you to provide them with a more personalized, and more pertinent, proposal. You may not get every one of the prospective customers that participated in stage 1 to move to stage 2. Let's assume for the sake of this example that 60% of customers progress to the next stage.

Stage 3 involves you presenting your product or service by way of demonstration. You use the information that you garnered in stage 2 to provide a personalized demonstration with examples that are pertinent to your customers' industry. Let's assume 40% of your prospects get to this stage.

Stage 4 involves you providing the prospect with a detailed commercial proposal that you are seeking their commitment on. It addresses the concerns that you have discussed. It shows your prospect how your solution addresses their problems, and it shows a return on the investment you are asking them to make, in a timeframe that is acceptable for that prospect. Let's assume that you close 50% of all customers who get to this point.

Your calculation therefore is as follows (for every 100 prospects, for ease of math)

Stage 1: 100 prospect engagement
Stage 2: 60 progress to this stage (i.e. 60%)
Stage 3: 40 progress to this stage (i.e. 40%)
Stage 4: 20 of these deals close (i.e. 50% of the 40 that progressed to stage 3)

This means that you have a pipeline closure rate of 20%, i.e. 20% of all prospects that enter your sales funnel will eventually become customers.

You can start to make these calculations more accurately if you have a well-defined sales process. This discipline in turn allows you to start to introduce some predictability into your business as you become more comfortable with the metrics that you see at each stage in your process.

By ratcheting up your pipeline generating activities you can see whether your assumptions are still valid, at scale. This allows you to make informed decisions about how and where you are investing your time and money, relative to the return you are getting. Another major benefit of this approach is you can start to refine the process, improving at each stage. The focus clearly is to determine what the triggers are for customers entering and exiting at each stage in the process.

If you can then address the issues that are causing people to exit (it may be price, the quality of your engagement, your salesperson, etc.), you can impact the volume of sales you close substantially. This is the ultimate aim of a well-defined sales process.

Chapter 6: Never lose alone

It might sound like a rather negative outlook to make this statement but losing alone is one of the cardinal sins of selling.

I first heard this expression from Mark Cranney, who at the time was heading up global sales for Opsware, a company subsequently bought by HP after a number of years of very significant sales growth, due in no small part to the strategy and direction of Mark.

If you are new to sales you may feel like it's your job, and yours alone, to go and secure business for your company. The reality could not be farther from the truth. The most successful salespeople I've seen are masters at creating virtual teams of people that collectively sell the capabilities of the company they represent.

Let's take a look at what this means. Let's assume you are selling a complex software solution. The likelihood is that you are selling to a technical buyer, but as I previously mentioned, they may have other influencers, or indeed they may not be the direct decision maker. At any point in time you may be required to engage and sell to, an economic buyer, a technical influencer, a project sponsor, a political influencer, operational contacts and your coach in the account, if you have one.

To cover the bases requires a team of people. Even if you felt that you knew who they were and could facilitate direct conversations with them, the reality is that not all of them want to hear what you have to say. They may, however, want to hear what a member of your team has to say.

Here's an example from my own experience. I've spent almost all of my sales career selling technically complex solutions to a largely technical audience.

I understood my product and prided myself on understanding the technical nuances of the market I was selling into, but it was rare that I would lead the technical discussion, even if I felt I was capable.

Instead I would make a point of engaging my technical expert. This achieves a number of things.

Firstly, it establishes another line of communication into your target customer. A technical contact will appreciate you taking the time to dedicate some technical resource to them.

It will also allow the technical influencer to ask the questions that are either hindering or supporting your likelihood of securing their business. Technically-minded folk, though brilliant, are also, in my experience, less likely to engage in these conversations with a salesperson, because they expect the salesperson to 'sell' to them. What this often means is that there's a suspicion on their part that the salesperson will simply tell them what they want to hear.

Even if this is not the case, hearing a technical response from a technical person is going to carry a lot more weight in the discussion than anything you are likely to contribute. One additional word of caution here. Make sure that you brief your technical support or pre-sales person appropriately to ensure that the words they use are carefully chosen to ensure that even challenging technical obstacles are discussed in a positive manner.

Technical pre-sales personnel are required to protect your business and ensure that whatever is committed to is deliverable and realistic from a technical perspective. As a result, they will naturally want to discuss the potential challenges that come with any project. This can occasionally come across as negative if the words and tone used by your pre-sales person are not tempered with an air of positivity.

This is particularly important when you are selling a technically complex solution so an agreement that 'challenges' should be noted and discussed offline is advisable.

This means when they are presented to a customer, the solution has been thought about and is no longer a challenge, but rather an opportunity for you to demonstrate value and provide further evidence supporting a decision to proceed.

Beyond the technical, there are other members of your team that you must align appropriately with their counterparts to ensure that you have ultimate coverage in your target account. If you are dealing at C-suite level, you should seek to mirror the executives that are involved in the decision making process. You will know who they are by being diligent with your questioning about the decision making process.

Who is involved?, Who is supporting the initiative?, Who can veto the decision? etc. With enough diligence in that process you should then seek to align the counterparts within your organization.

Think about it in these terms. If you are talking with someone who does the same job as you, has the same pressures as you, often the same day to day experiences as you, you have an instant shared appreciation for that person. It's human nature. By ensuring that you align your team with peers on the team of decision makers at your target account, you greatly improve your chances of securing their business.

There are lots of other reasons that this approach makes sense. Engaging your target with representatives from your team in the areas of technology, finance, legal, project management, etc. demonstrates a form of commitment from the client. You should be concerned if you are recommending that these meetings happen and the buyer does not want to participate.

This shows a lack of engagement and should be viewed as a challenge in your sales process that needs to be overcome.

Conversely, if a client is happily engaging in these meetings, provided you have the right people connected with each other, your chances of securing that business increase exponentially.

With these connections in place, your job becomes more complex, so you need to ensure that you become the centralized point of command and control in the account. You should be intimately aware of the content of any meetings or calls that your virtual team is having. Each of these should be either established by you, or verified by you as being appropriate to move the sale forward. If meetings are happening without your knowledge, you are not in control, either of the process or the communications that are inevitably happening.

Awareness of what contact and communication is taking place within your target account is absolutely key in the team-based sale.

Another major benefit of the team-based sale is that you have additional 'eyes and ears' in the account. I have often recommended that my technical pre-sales person spend some time on-site with the target client so we could gain a greater understanding of the problems they faced.

Where this offer is accepted you have the opportunity to gain valuable insight on the issues faced by your client. You also have an opportunity to determine exactly what is going on with the team, the challenges they face, what they think of the incumbent solution (if there is one), what they think of their boss and the strategy of the business and so forth.

This may seem like idle chat in many cases, but it's valuable to determine if the person you are dealing with is respected in their business.

You can also determine if their star is on the rise internally, if they have the authority to make the decision they claim they can make, etc. All of these insights, to use an artistic metaphor, are further brush-strokes on the canvas.

By collating these across multiple areas within your target account, pretty soon you will see a picture emerge. This picture is either a work of art, or depending on the insights gained, could be a messy scrawl that begs the question – is there a purchasing process or decision making process in play at all, or are you selling to a tire-kicker? If the picture that emerges is not positive, don't worry, it's as important to get to no as it is to get to yes in sales, often more so if your market is commoditized.

So the lesson here is to ensure that when selling in a complex environment, with a number of people with differing interests making the decision, make sure that you align your team with theirs. Doing so will ensure you have the bases covered and more importantly, have insights into their respective progress as you get nearer to a decision.

Bottom Line: The salesperson who sells alone, loses alone. Never lose alone.

Chapter 7: The sales mindset.

In this chapter I want to talk a little bit about the importance of mindset when it comes to sales. What follows are some of the most important themes to keep front of mind if you wish to be successful in sales.

People buy from people

We spend such a large amount of our time on this earth at work. We spend a third of most days surrounded by people we work with and for. For a prospective customer they are not just evaluating your product or service they are evaluating you. Consciously or subconsciously they are asking themselves 'can I work with this person?, do I like them?, are they genuine?, do they believe in their product or service?' This is human nature. Trust is the first hurdle you must overcome when seeking to establish a relationship.

This relationship-building ability is often described by others as being a 'people person'. Not everyone has the capacity or inclination to be a 'people person' but it's pretty important in sales. This is not about becoming someone you are not, or pretending to like someone when you don't. It's about making the connection between human behavior and the ways in which our behavior towards the person we are selling to, is perceived. It's well understood that people categorize you within seconds of meeting you and whether that perception is positive or negative has a lot to do with how you interact with people and of course the 'first impressions' you give people when they meet you.

This is under your control to a very large extent, and apart from the obvious friendly, open, approachable and professional image that anyone who is selling should have, there is an element of adaptation that's required depending on the person sitting in front of you.

As a general rule, the more you speak with, interact with and listen to people, the more appreciation you get for the nuances and in some cases, the peculiarities, of people.

Personally, I was never great at small talk, nor was I a big sports guy so much of the small talk that I associated with sales was dispensed with and replaced with showing a real interest in people and what made them who they were. I typically got a little closer to customers than many of my counterparts because the nature of our conversations tended to be a little more personal in nature. Not in a contrived manner, but as I knew little or nothing about sports, I was forced to lead the conversation in a different direction. What started out in my mind as a potential weakness became one of my strengths.

The key point here is to take the time to appreciate and listen to the prospect that you are dealing with, as a person – not as a prospect. They have their own life, their own motivations. Often, having an appreciation for these elements of a person can make the difference when it comes to shaping the proposition that you create for them.

If your contact is an analytical person who is risk averse, your sales approach will be very different to a person who is actively seeking to advance their career. In the first instance, introducing a broader team that shows bench-depth in your company and addresses many of the concerns that the prospect has may advance your sales proposition. For others, leveraging your senior execs to meet with your contact and their boss may help the career oriented prospect get some face-time with their superiors, and provide them with an opportunity to shine.

Taking the time to consider the person rather than the prospect will bear fruit and will help you be more successful.

The key take-away from this point, however, is that irrespective of the type of person you are dealing with, make it a positive experience for them.

Be solution-focused rather than problem-focused

The process of selling is challenging and you should expect to be faced with issues on a regular basis. What's important however is that when you are faced with a challenge, you must focus on finding the solution, rather than getting fixated on the problem.

This may seem like semantics but here's an example of what I mean.

A few years into my sales career I was working on a deal with a large bank. I felt we were reasonably well placed. I had a good rapport with the middle management team and had good coverage in the account. Things were progressing well.

I sat down one day to map out the organizational structure, to make sure I had all the bases covered, and once completed I felt we were lacking coverage in the senior management team. We didn't have direct contact with the overall project sponsor (a rookie mistake). I identified the person and reached out to their office. I was cut off by their personal assistant who suggested that I send her an email and if Steve (not his real name) was free he'd call me back.

A day or two passed and after another couple of calls it was clear that Steve's personal assistant (Sheena) was screening me out. This was a problem. Not only did it mean that I wasn't getting any facetime with Steve, but worse, it potentially meant we were not as well placed as I had thought. I focused on how I was going to get some time with Steve.

With some digging I discovered that Steve was speaking at a financial services conference a couple of weeks later. I convinced my boss at the time that this was a conference that I needed to be at.

I bought a ticket and turned up on the day Steve was due to speak. On arrival I spent some time trying to track Steve down.

It turned out that Steve would be arriving just a few minutes before he was due to speak, so I sat in the auditorium towards the front of the audience. Steve was ushered in just before his speaking slot. He gave his speech and then opened the floor up for questions. With a roving microphone in the audience my hand shot up to ask a question. Eventually the mic came to me. I introduced myself and my company. Thinking quickly, I came up with what I felt was both a thought provoking and relevant question for the audience, which Steve answered.

I thanked him and before handing the mic back to the assistant said 'I'd love to grab two minutes after your speech to talk a little bit further about that'. Steve said, 'yes of course,' nodded and smiled. That was it. I had two minutes and that was enough for me to explain to Steve that I was attending the event as it was important for me to understand more about his company, as myself and my team were working with his team. I added that I appreciated that a hotel conference room probably wasn't the best place for us to have a detailed discussion but asked if I could call Sheena (his PA) to grab an hour of his time to give him an update on our proposal and approach to make sure we were aligned with what he wanted. He agreed. I had my meeting.

The moral here is that I wasn't fixated on the problem, I was fixated on finding a solution. This is a distinction that the very best salespeople make. Sometimes it comes naturally, but even if it doesn't, stick these words on a post-it and place it somewhere prominent so you've got a constant reminder 'Solutions - not problems'.

No room for negativity

Have you ever spent an extended period of time with a negative person? A person who constantly sees the downside, questions everything, and is essentially a glass-half-empty type of person.

It's exhausting. Oh, and by the way, it achieves nothing – zero. Some people seem to thrive on filling their days with it, and ultimately, achieve nothing more than making themselves miserable and standing in the way of progress rather than helping to contribute to it.

It's part of life that things go wrong. I'm not suggesting that everything is always perfect, but how you react to negativity is what helps define your life, and in sales this is particularly true. The under-achievers that I've encountered in sales always had an excuse for why they were not meeting target, or why their deals were taking so long to close. The list of excuses was endless.

In truth, what I saw was a lot of self-fulfilling prophecies as the individuals concerned often lacked the self-belief that they needed to be successful and it showed in their interactions with prospects and colleagues and in the quality of their work.

Personally, I do everything I can to avoid negativity. I don't read the news, or consume it online – the world and the media is full of negative commentary – that's often what makes it newsworthy.

By osmosis I still manage to get enough news to know what's happening in the world, but the trade-off between avoiding negativity and surrounding myself with positivity is one I'll easily make, and do every day.

If you are reading this chapter and can't quite relate to the 'always keep it positive' message, then it may be because a lot of the negativity we experience in life comes from our biggest critic – ourselves. We have an internal dialogue with ourselves that re-enforces many of the negative perceptions we have of ourselves.

For example, when we say 'That's too expensive' when we are quoting for our product or service what we should really be saying is 'I am going to sell the value'. It's a subtle but powerful change that we need to make and comes back to being solution focused versus problem focused.

When we change the dialogue that we have with ourselves internally, we change the reality for ourselves externally. Try it for a month. You will be amazed at the changes it brings about.

If you are going to be a world-class salesperson, there are no shortcuts. You have to work hard and be consistent, not just externally with your prospects, but also with your colleagues.

As mentioned previously, sales is a team sport and if your fellow teammates don't feel the positivity and the belief that you can win, and worse still, they know that you don't believe in yourself enough to win, it's game over. Go get another job, or change your attitude.

The attitude you have will show in your work and in your results. If you maintain a positive outlook, have a strong work ethic, believe you can win and go to work every day with that belief you will be successful.

I have an unshakable belief in my ability to succeed. I believe it, I live it, it shows, and others believe it too as I reach those goals and beyond them.

I believe 100% in myself, not just when I succeed but arguably, more importantly when I fail. That's the challenge. Do you have enough strength of character, enough willpower, enough self-belief when you have failed, to pick yourself up, get back in the saddle and genuinely, deeply feel that you will succeed? I do, and in truth the degree to which I believe it has grown stronger as I've become older and more experienced.

I should also state that I have, as I am writing this book, experienced one of the largest failures of my career to date, and despite this I genuinely feel more powerful and more likely to succeed further than I have at any other time in my life. Can you say the same?

It is the challenge and how you deal with it that defines you, not the failure itself. Failure is an inherent ingredient in success. For example, we do not leave the comfort of the womb and immediately start to walk. We learn, after many attempts, bruises and knocks how to walk and so it is with sales. You will lose deals, you will be outsold, you will be blindsided with decisions, you will be there simply to make up the numbers, you will be short-changed, you will have deals die before you get ink on paper. This happens in sales.

I'm not suggesting that you take all of this lying down. Quite the opposite, I'm suggesting that it is because this happens and you learn and grow as a result, that you will become a better sales person.

You will respond well to each challenge, you will take lessons from it and you will not let it happen again.

There's room for a little disappointment. That's natural, but only to the extent that feeling bad acts as a catalyst to getting back in the game and proving you have what it takes to 'right that wrong' and start building towards success again.
In the words of Michael Jordon, you need to appreciate the shots you took that missed as much as the ones that made the basket.

Positivity is contagious

If you spend time with inherently positive people you'll find, in time that you become more positive. There are a number of reasons for this, but central to this change is the observation that life is easier when you are positive. It's easier because you see things differently. Where before you saw challenges, now you see opportunity. This is quite a simple concept but it's not always easy for people to make that change.

Positivity in the context of selling is not about blind positivity, you have got to put the work in to support your positivity.
A poorly written proposal submitted by a supremely positive person is still a poorly written proposal.

Your thoughts and your actions should complement each other, thus creating a positivity cycle that is self-sustaining. By putting the work in and being positive, you create an environment where positive outcomes become possible.

People recognize hard work, and they appreciate positivity. In sales you need both to attract the support of others. For your internal support you rely on work colleagues to help you draft your proposal or presentation.

You rely on executive management to support your sales efforts when you ask them to meet with their counterparts in your prospects organization and you rely on your product management or service support team to be there to help you win that business.

This is the first audience you must build trust with and by working hard and remaining steadfastly positive, even in the midst of adversity, you can gain and maintain that trust.

With a strong, trusting, positive team you can achieve a great deal. When you engage a prospective customer in this manner, this positivity is contagious and should not be underestimated in terms of its importance when it comes to making their decision. In fact, I've made it a habit of asking customers why they chose us whenever a deal has closed so I could ensure we recognize what customers saw in our proposals that stood out.

When you put aside some of the technical differentiators that some of the companies I've worked for have had, there have a been a great number of deals that I and my teams have closed over the years, where customers have commented that the way our team worked to support them was a key differentiator.

You can only achieve that kind of dynamic when positivity abounds within the team and the key take away here is that it starts with one person. You. Never underestimate the power of positivity.

Chapter 8: Where's the value? – building your proposition.

One of the most important elements of your sales process is your value proposition. You may ask yourself what it is that you are trying to sell? A more appropriate question is, what is it that the customer is seeking to buy? Let me explain the difference.

You may believe that you are selling a software product, or a professional service but this is not how your customer views the world. They have engaged with you, and some of your competitors because they have a challenge, perhaps many challenges that they are seeking to address.

Part of your role as a professional salesperson is to understand these challenges and determine how, what you and your company have to offer, aligns with solving those challenges. You also need to consider the possibility that your prospect doesn't fully understand all of their challenges, or may be dealing with just the symptoms of an issue rather than the underlying problem.

To build your value proposition you should think about it across a number of dimensions. For example, if your company provides software that helps businesses manage their warehouse stock more effectively for faster turnaround on orders, it's going to be useful to think about who and what departments are likely to have an interest in this initiative.

I typically start by looking at the first dimension, across a company, so in this example clearly the logistics and shipping department are going to have interest.

The sales department may have interest because it will now be able to ship product more quickly, allowing it to be more responsive, thereby helping to win more business.

The finance department will be interested given the potential cash flow implications of turning over stock more efficiently.

The COO will be interested because this increases operational efficiency. The list continues. This is a departmental perspective and typically we are looking horizontally at the business, i.e. by business function.

I then start to look the second dimension (vertically within each department) to determine the specific alignment of this project with business objectives, strategic initiatives and corporate imperatives within each department. What starts to emerge when you do this is a clearer picture of where your project sits in terms of importance. This is a great time to ask some critical questions such as:

- Who has an interest in the success of this project?
- Who has anything to lose if this project progresses?
- What departments have the most to gain from a successful project?
- Are there other competing projects that might jeopardize this project?
- Does this project contribute to one or more of the strategic imperatives for this year / next year?
- What happens if you do nothing?

That last question in particular is really powerful. The question is designed to determine whether this project really needs to happen or not. Is there a compelling reason why the company should do anything? If there isn't a compelling reason for a project to progress you can be pretty sure it won't, and your time and effort will have been wasted.

It is this level of questioning that will help as you work to build your proposition. The information gathered should act as the foundation of your proposal and the quality of your proposal will be directly proportional to the effort and attention to detail that you gave to this discovery phase.

As previously mentioned, you should spend the majority of your time listening to the responses and the nuances of terms used, intonation, and the percentage of time spent speaking about each issue, as this often helps you understand what is most important to a prospect.

Once you've mapped out the two dimensions I mentioned earlier, you need to map your resources across each key departmental contact. Align your technical resources with the tech team, your commercial discussions with the financial contacts, your operational team with their operations contacts and so forth.

Personally, I am a bit of a control freak so I make a point of being at every one of the meetings with these teams. It's important to me that I have a holistic view of what is being said to my prospect by different members of the team, but also it allows me to sit in these meetings and observe a great deal. How is the tech team responding to our answers? How are the operations team responding to our support and project related discussions? etc.

The reactions, often very subtle, give you insight into the support or opposition that your proposal is likely to receive. Pay close attention to people's body language as this is a significant sign of their interest or otherwise, I've found.

In each of the departmental meetings you then want to align their interests with a corporate objective, or a strategic imperative for the business. This is the second dimension I spoke about earlier. If you can't do this, then you should ask yourself how important this initiative is for the business.

Not every departments' objectives will align perfectly with the other's but for a project to succeed there should be common alignment around the most significant objectives or imperatives. This is how projects happen.

They gain broad-based support and they are aligned with something that is important for the business.

If this is not becoming apparent in the course of your discussions you should be worried. Don't be afraid to make the observation to your contacts that while they seem to find the project of interest, it doesn't seem to be aligned with a particularly important initiative in the business.

Test their response. If you are wrong, the worst that will happen is that they clarify exactly why the project is so important and you have a nugget for your proposal document.

If they struggle to answer, that's a red flag and should be viewed as a potential challenge for you and your sales process. In other words, the opportunity is not what it appears.

As you participate in these meetings I've found it useful to make notes of the key themes that strike you. The themes that emerge may be different for each stakeholder (IT, Finance, Operations etc.), but it will be important that the needs of each stakeholder are reflected in the proposal you provide.

A good way to think about the proposal is to work back from an 'Ideal proposal'. Here's what I mean. If you can picture each of the internal stakeholders reading the proposal and nodding vigorously at the section of the proposal that addresses their concerns then you have achieved a great deal.

To achieve this means you must listen intently to the issues they describe during your discovery sessions. I refer to them as themes because I believe that most people read a proposal or observe a presentation and what they are left with are a series of themes.

Once you are clear on what the themes are for each department, you should seek to align them clearly within your proposal. For example, if our proposal was focused on warehouse efficiency, and this aligned with a strategic imperative for growth in your prospects business you might have the theme aligned with this strategic imperative. Under the heading of 'growth' in your proposal you would have internal beneficiaries listed as the operations team who stated that stock turnover efficiency was a major issue for them.

You would have growth as a theme for sales who stated that target achievement and revenue growth was a major theme for them.

You would have growth as a theme for the technology team who had technology refresh as an objective for this year. You get the idea.

Once you have completed the departmental stakeholder reviews for your discovery phase, what will emerge is a picture that reflects their needs from the project, and the ways in which these needs align with an objective or imperative.

I also find it useful to use the customers' strategic imperatives alongside these themes and then work back from there to build out my proposal. By talking the customer's language, you can help them create the connection between their objectives / imperatives and your solution. This is the central objective of your value proposition. Your value is in helping them to achieve or exceed these objectives.

Another point to note during your discovery sessions is the potential that your prospect may be missing some of the value that you can bring. Often prospects are so caught up in their day to day jobs that they don't see some of the benefits immediately.

You should view it as your job to ensure that every single benefit, no matter how small is made clear to them.

As an example, if, as part of your discovery process you identify savings of $20,000 per week as a result of warehouse efficiency, another way of looking at this is that the company is losing $20,000 for every week that they delay in moving forward with your solution. This 'opportunity cost' could quite easily be missed by the customer as they may not necessarily be thinking in these terms.

You may also uncover additional benefits that are not apparent to individual stakeholders as internal communication between the stakeholders may not be as open as you might expect.

The main point here is ensuring that you drive your own benefits statements in your proposal as well as being directed by the benefits that the customer expects to see.

I should also mention that when you create the value proposition element of your proposal, you should ensure that you give the benefits the correct weighting. This is based on your knowledge not just of the monetary value you bring, but on the strategic value to the stakeholders you are working with, and their relative importance in the decision making process.

What I mean by this is that while you may save a great deal of money for the operations team, the strategic imperative of revenue increase (rather than cost saving) may be more important and your proposal and presentation should reflect this.

If you've done your job correctly, your value proposition will tick the boxes for all of the major stakeholders and they should feel that their interests are represented.

They should feel that their voice has been heard and the solution will help them achieve the objectives and imperatives that they shared with you.

This discovery phase is the foundation upon which you will build your sales campaign so it is vitally important that you give it the attention it deserves. 70% of your time should be spent in this phase to make sure that you truly understand what is important to the prospect. They will appreciate it and your work will pay dividends when it comes to the latter part of your sales process.

Chapter 9: The right stuff. What is takes to make it in sales.

Before we get further into the detail of sales and the process of selling I want to take some time to discuss some personal beliefs that I have about sales and what makes a good salesperson.

As you read this chapter I encourage you to do a little soul-searching and to ask yourself, if you have these qualities, or the desire to develop them. Having worked with hundreds of salespeople over the course of my career I've been surprised at how wide the spectrum of salespeople can be in terms of approach, delivery style and more.

What I've not been surprised by is what traits they have in common and this chapter is designed to explore these traits and to share my thoughts on the relative importance of each. You can use these as a kind of yard-stick for your own suitability for sales, or as a means of identifying areas that could perhaps do with some examination or improvement.

Equally if you are in the position of recruiting salespeople, these are the traits that I would suggest are most important to look for when hiring. It should be noted that these traits are not in any order of importance as I feel they are all integral parts of a great salesperson.

Work Ethic

The degree of comfort that you have with hard work I believe will be reflected in the results you achieve as a salesperson. For those on the outside, sales often looks easy, glamorous even, but the reality is very different.

You fly very close to the ground for the majority of your career in sales and while occasionally you can soar like a fighter pilot after a great win, you may also crash and burn if you are not working hard to keep your sales process under control.

All great salespeople have, in my experience an unrelenting desire to work; however it's not a chore for them. It is a by-product of their desire to win and to prove themselves.

Work ethic is not about blindly punching in extra hours or working on weekends. It's about starting with the basics, working hard on those, then progressing to the next level, working on that and so on. In practical terms this means working hard on understanding your market, understanding your product, understanding your competitors, understanding their strengths and weaknesses, understanding what tools you have at your disposal internally and understanding how to convey what differentiates your product or service from your competitors. These are some of the basics.

You shouldn't meet with a single prospective customer until you've got these nailed. This is the 'wax-on, wax-off' approach to learning that takes a strong work ethic to master. There are no real shortcuts that you can take. You need to put the work in, to get the results.

Attitude

There's a saying about attitude that goes 'Attitude is everything. Life is 10% what happens to you and 90% how you react to it'. I couldn't agree more. A great salesperson sees opportunity where others see adversity. In sales you are presented with obstacles every step of the way. That's why they call it 'selling' and not 'order taking'.

Given that you are presented with a series of obstacles in the sales process, how you react to these obstacles determines your success as a salesperson. You can view an obstructive PA as an obstacle, or you can check that approach off the list and try another. I'm with Thomas Edison when it comes to my reaction to things that don't work. I'm just one step closer to discovering what will work. This is attitude.

We have all witnessed people who have a defeatist attitude. They look at opportunities to confirm their negative beliefs. They are the people who go to great lengths to explain why something didn't work rather than channeling that energy into finding out what will work. They accept the obstacles as just that, obstacles, rather than expected challenges that exist to be overcome.

Competitiveness

Personally, I always ask any salesperson that I interview what they have done competitively in their lives and to what standard they have progressed.

I've worked with former Olympians, track and field athletes who have represented their country and competitive mountain climbers and despite the difference in their respective sports, the characteristics of the person are very similar. It's not just the competiveness that I look for – that's often apparent, it's the stories of how they've responded in difficult situations.

Perhaps they've lost a race and returned the following year to win the title. Perhaps it's the story of sacrifice that they endured to reach the heights of success in their chosen sport. Perhaps it's just sharing the stories of what it took for them to achieve their own personal victory in a chosen competitive field, but in each case, I've listened to their response to determine how competitive they are.

The reason I feel this is important is this. People who have competed in their early years and progressed to achieve something in their chosen sport have an innate competitiveness that, in my experience is harder to foster later in life.

In addition, they will have seen the benefits of putting in the hard work, the hours of training, the blood, sweat and tears that comes from competing at a high level and therefore will have established that connection between hard work and a successful outcome.

Consistency

The very best salespeople are not those who have the occasional win, they are the salespeople who demonstrate that they are consistently able to close business.

There's a saying 'a stopped clock is still accurate twice a day' and so it is with certain salespeople. They've had success with a bluebird deal (one that fell in their lap) and they mistakenly believe that if they hang around long enough they will get another one. These are the salespeople whose resume reads like a random list of companies with the tenure at each lasting between 9 and 12 months.

Now don't get me wrong. An element of job movement is to be expected in a salesperson's résumé. They may be genuinely headhunted to move to a competitor or have valid reasons for wanting to move. Generally speaking, if I receive a résumé with less than two years at each company I view it with an element of concern – that's just me.

What I am looking for is consistency in their ability to deliver results, and that takes time. If you are constantly moving, you can't easily demonstrate consistency.

Those that do show consistency in their work record and target achievement are far more preferable to me as there is a pretty direct link between tenure and target achievement in sales.

If they weren't achieving target, they wouldn't have lasted that long. That's the nature of sales and the byproduct of having a pretty binary assessment of performance. You've either hit target or you have not. Whether you are a salesperson or hiring a salesperson – strive for consistency.

Intelligence (versus academic ability)

This is perhaps one of the most significant elements of the evaluation for me. First, let's start by defining intelligence in sales. Intelligence in sales for me is about demonstrating that you have the ability to overcome obstacles, to determine the correct sales strategy, and to evaluate and correctly deduce where you have weaknesses in your sales campaign.

It's also about being able to identify the key individuals in your target companies' org chart, to create a coherent and well written proposal, to articulate a clear and differentiated value proposition for your targeted account and so forth.

It's part street smarts, part aptitude, part hustle, but importantly, it's about ensuring that you are busy doing the right things to move your opportunity forward. It's quite easy to be busy doing all the wrong things if you don't have the intelligence to know the difference.

Personal character.

Personal character is something that is built from early childhood and continues to develop, either positively or negatively as time progresses.

To determine personal character is difficult in the context of an interview but by taking the time to get to know the individual by asking them about non-work related interests, hobbies and activities it's amazing how much people reveal about themselves.

I like to ask people about their background, their upbringing, their interests, what they do outside of work, any charitable work they are involved in, the types of books they read, etc. This helps to reveal their personal character a little more.

I am looking for admirable qualities such as a willingness to learn, an ability to adapt, team player qualities, a desire to progress personally and grow personally. The elements of a person's character that are likely to be comfortable in the environment in which I am asking them to work.

Culturally, the character of the individual must be a fit for your company or team, so the more time you spend understanding and gaining an appreciation for their personal character, the more likely you are to find a good fit for both you and the salesperson.

I've worked with some great salespeople over the past 20 years but I will also admit to having hired a few bad ones. The characteristics that I have mentioned in this chapter are those that I feel are important based on both my positive and negative experiences in this regard and should be viewed as leading indicators to help you in your self-assessment or your evaluation of a potential new hire.

Whatever you do, hire very carefully. A great salesperson can be transformative for your business but a bad salesperson can close more doors than they open.

Chapter 10: The org-chart. Who's who in the zoo?

Depending on the nature of what you are selling and who you are selling to, you may need an organizational chart to help you navigate the company you are dealing with.

Thankfully, with the advent of online tools such as LinkedIn getting to know who works at your target company, how you might connect with them and how other employees are connected is easier than ever. Surprisingly however, many salespeople don't take the time to research this.

In this chapter, we will examine the importance of understanding the organizational chart and categorizing the key individuals on the chart that you need to be engaged with as part of the sales process.

An understanding of this is most important when you are involved in selling to large enterprises. There is a complexity that comes with enterprise sales that you really need to appreciate if you are going to be successful. It starts by understanding the names and roles of everyone that is going to be important in bringing the sale to closure.

Here are some of the roles that you might find in a typical sales engagement for a tech company trying to sell to a large corporate.

Executive sponsor.
This is the person who has executive responsibility for making this project happen. They typically sit towards the top of your org chart and ultimately need to be satisfied with the recommendations of their team before any contract is awarded.

Technical sponsor.
For large companies you are dealing with a technical environment that may be decades or more in the making and has inherent complexity that you need to be aware of before proposing your technical solution.

In these large companies the technical sponsor is typically part of the CTO or CIO's office, if not the CTO or CIO directly. It is their job to ensure that any technology that comes into their world plays nicely with everything else they have, and of course, meets strict standards as they relate to privacy, security, reliability, and in many cases auditability for compliance purposes.

Financial evaluator.
When selling to a large enterprise, you can expect that there is a financial evaluation that takes place. This can consist of a number of stages and elements but can be summarized as an internal assessment of the rate of return. Put simply this means, for every dollar the company spends they generate X dollars either in increased sales, or decreased costs, often both.

If you don't know what that internal rate of return is, you need to find it. In many instances if you don't meet that basic test, your proposal will not make it past the financial checks and your deal is dead. In other instances, your deal may meet the internal rate of return; however, a competing project may deliver a higher rate of return and again, your deal is dead. For this and many other reasons, you need to know who the financial sponsor is and the metrics they are using to evaluate your proposal.

Coach:
A coach is someone who gives you insights into the buying and decision making process.

You may not know who they are at first but after engaging with the prospective company they typically make themselves known by sharing some information that is valuable to you in the sale process. Having a coach is invaluable as it means you have someone to help you navigate the minefield of the prospects company.

The larger the company the more important it is to have a coach as they can help you avoid the political challenges that often come with purchasing decisions, particularly if the deal is strategically important to them. I've been involved in deals that have had more political maneuverings than an episode of Game of Thrones so having a coach in those deals has been extremely important.

Think of a coach as a GPS for your deal. They help you navigate the challenges of getting a deal from the initial opening right through to closure. They keep a constant lookout for obstacles or delays and help you avoid or navigate your way around them, and they provide lots of 'points of interest' that help you achieve your objective of closing the deal.

So with all of these benefits, why wouldn't you want a coach involved in your deal? Well, it's a question you need to ask yourself – Do you have a coach today in each of your deals? If you don't, then you are at a distinct disadvantage. Think about what that means. You don't have a single person in the account rooting for you, wanting you to win that business? That's an issue.

So the question that you should now be asking yourself is how do I get a coach in the account. Well, the first thing to note about coaches is that they don't always reveal themselves immediately.

They may not even realize that they want you to win the business until they make a connection between what you are trying to achieve and what they are trying to achieve.

Here's an example from a deal that I closed a number of years back. It was with a multi-national financial services company. I was working with the London office, which was the headquarters for the company but they had a very large US operation. In fact, the US operation was almost five times larger in terms of business volume than the UK operation but for historical reasons London was the centre of power. I was engaged with the COO of the UK team and had been working with his team for a couple of months. The US team had flown over to London for a couple of meetings but were very challenging to read. It was hard to put my finger on what it was at the time.

I remember thinking the US team were agreeable but not fully engaged and certainly not to the same extent as their European counterparts. I was part of a global software company and had tried to get my US colleagues involved in the deal under the auspices of providing local support for the decision making process. Our prospect politely declined explaining that they would be taking direction from their UK counterparts.

I can recall vividly the choice of words that they used at our meeting in London when I offered the support and the way in which they said we will be 'taking direction' from the UK somehow didn't ring true for me. The meeting finished and they returned back to the US promising that they would follow up with questions within a few days.

True to their word, 3-4 days later they emailed a couple of pages of questions. As I read through the questions it was clear to me that they were planted by a competitor.

The questions were very deliberately focused on some of the areas of our solution that were not as well developed as a competitive product. This is a tactic that I have used many times myself so I could recognize what was happening.

The US team were evaluating a competitive product and it was clear that they were coaching the competitor as the questions were so pointed and deliberately designed to undermine our offering.

I spoke with the COO in London and explained what I thought was happening, as diplomatically as I could. He immediately opened up, explaining that his counterpart in the US was politically motivated and was working to bring more of the 'power base' to the US and making their own decisions was the first step in this process. This wasn't widely known but my contact was keenly aware of this fact.

He proceeded to explain that our solution, while not perfect, had all of the critical elements for the business. We supported multiple languages. We provided a centralized global support desk which was essential when things went wrong. We had a great deal more domain expertise in the financial services sector than our competitor and our executive team and his executive team were very closely aligned and worked well together.

For these reasons he felt we were a good fit for the business; however, for due diligence purposes, he was eager to ensure that we respond to the questions and ensure that he had comparative information for our competitor. He said that he would speak with his US counterpart and that any competitive offering would be discussed and compared openly.

To that end, he spoke with the US team and agreed that there would be a joint evaluation of the offerings over a one-month period with a series of technical, commercial and operational team meetings to determine and compare the appropriateness of each solution.

Armed with the elements of the solution that were important to the company, we focused all of our efforts on the multi-lingual nature of our product, the 'follow-the-sun' support that we offered and ensured that our executives and their counterparts in the prospects company met regularly over the evaluation period.

The COO 'coached' me before every session and even reviewed and critiqued my presentations before each session to ensure that we were adequately prepared. In his opening comments at a number of the sessions he reiterated the elements of the ideal solution that were paramount in their decision making process and sought the US teams' agreement that this was the case.

This coaching was pivotal in our pitches as it neutralized our competitor and disarmed the US team who had agreed on the elements of the solution that were most important, thereby weakening the competitor's offering.

So the moral of this story is this. If you can align your solution with the needs of the business and the motivations and aspirations of the right people, you are in a great position to win.

By aligning with the personal motivations of an individual, you create an ally, and that ally will want you to win. If they want you to win, they may act as a coach, though, not in all cases, but this is something you should strive for.

So to answer the question about how to attract a coach, you must start by understanding the motivations of your contacts in the account. A coach may come from any of the levels of the organization but typically, the more senior the better as they will help you navigate the most perilous element of large-scale strategic projects – the political landscape.

Operational owner:
This is, as the name suggests, the person who is going to have to live with whatever product or service you provide once the sale has been closed.

It's important to make sure that you are closely aligned with this person and fully understand their needs. In many instances this person, while not the final decision maker will play a significant part in it.

They may not have complete freedom to say 'Yes' but have the ability to say 'No'. They are typically middle-management and are the day to day user or consumer of your product or service. When you first engage with this person, make sure that you spend the majority of your time asking open questions, and crucially, make sure that you listen closely to their answers.

If you are asking good open questions such as 'Tell me about the ideal solution to the challenges you've got', you are going to gain really valuable insight into what is important for the user and the more space you give them to talk, more often than not, the more they will share with you.

You may think you've seen and heard it all before, but often it's the little gem of information they share with you in the initial couple of conversations that proves valuable.

If you are attuned, you'll pick up on what they are saying, and often, just as important, what they are not saying. For example, I remember distinctly, sitting in one of my first meetings as a salesperson and coming away from the meeting thinking the individual really did not like their boss. They spent a great deal of the meeting criticizing the way things had been done in the past and they were focused on changing it.

Over a post-meeting beer, I asked one of his colleagues if there was an issue with my contact and his boss. They responded – 'He wants his job, and he'll get it as his [boss's] days are numbered'. This was valuable insight. This was more than just another project. My contact saw what we were doing as a means of progressing his career.

That was his motivation, and actually resulted in my contact also becoming my coach in the account.

Another thing to note with operational owners is the power and importance of references. If you can align your operational owner with similar operational owners in your customer base who are happy to vouch for what you do, that will give your prospect some additional reassurance.

Hearing from a person faced with the same challenges as they have on a day to day basis is a powerful testimony. Make sure that you time this appropriately. You must first fully understand what your prospect is looking for before introducing them to an existing customer. If you don't fully understand their needs, you may introduce them to a customer whose experience of your product or service is not appropriately aligned with your prospects needs.

This is a good way to lose a deal so make sure you've got that understanding before you play matchmaker with the reference. Make sure you check out the chapter on reference selling for more detail.

Chapter 11: Know your competitors.

The great Chinese military leader Sun Tzu who once wrote (in his book The Art of War), 'Every battle is won before it is fought'. What he meant by this is that by having an understanding of your enemy you can create a set of circumstances that means they cannot be successful. The same is true in sales, to an extent. In other words, the better you understand your competition, the better prepared you can be for the daily fight that involves you competing with them.

Now, you may say to yourself, I know my competitors, I know what makes me better, what makes me or my product stand out from the crowd. This is not the issue. The issue is, do you know what is important for your customer to understand when they are evaluating the competitive landscape? This is the art of war.

Let's look at this topic, not as a war of attrition, but rather as a war of strategies. It used to amaze me when I worked with some more junior salespeople, how much time they spent in a back and forth with their prospects about how much better their product was, compared to the competition.

They would repeat ad-nauseam, we are better because of A,B,C,D and E. The competitor didn't have F,G,H,J and K. It was almost like a mantra. What was missing in these discussions was an appreciation of what the customer viewed as important to them. If you know what is important to your prospective customer, you can easily deposition your competitors. Let me illustrate by way of an example.

In recent years I was working with a company that sold solutions in the financial services sector. They were a mid-size company operating in a specialized field.

We had engaged with a prospect who operated across the U.S. and Europe and represented a multi-million-dollar opportunity to the company in question.

The prospect had grown by acquisition and as a result has acquired a number of technologies that competed directly with that of the company I was working with. They wanted to consolidate and were progressing down the path of one of the incumbent providers, who also happened to be the world's largest provider of this type of solution.

Over the course of several months, I had met with key members of their executive team, from their COO right down to some of their regional European directors. It was clear that this company was concerned with providing a more personalized experience for their customers, so I noted this as a key requirement.

A number of other comments were made about the desire to personalize the product to take account of various cultural differences that existed across their global entities, and of course there were language variations to further consider.

When the time came for us to have more detailed discussions with the senior executive, we prepared a demonstration that encompassed all of this. We paid great attention to detail to ensure that regional variations were obvious and we had multiple demonstration versions of the product to show them. We spent a lot of time helping them to come to their own conclusions that what to begin with were 'nice-to-have's' were now 'must-have's. I refer to these as competitive landmines.

If you manage this process correctly, you should be able to deposition your competition before they engage. By firstly understanding what is important to the prospect and then overlaying and having them prioritize what is unique about your product you will have created significant challenges for your competitors.

I've personally found that having a primary competitor in mind when evaluating how well positioned you are in a sales cycle.

I've always found it motivating to assume that if I allowed it, my competitor was always one step ahead of me, they were always working to get higher up the tree in terms of the decision maker. Sales is Darwinian in nature. It literally is the act of adaptation and evolution of your sales process and style of selling in an effort to prevail, to survive. If you are not adapting, you will die, and in time your company will die with you. The fact that you have a competitor should therefore be viewed not as a disadvantage, but rather it should be viewed as something to be exploited and built upon. Let me give you a further example to illustrate the point.

In my early sales career, I was working for a company in the telecoms space. Our primary competitor was a company called Rockwell. They were part of a global conglomerate that had commercial interests that ranged from aerospace to satellite components and a great deal in between. It had tens of thousands of employees across the globe. It was a giant compared to the company that I worked for. By contrast, my company was approximately 1500 people predominantly in the UK and USA.

At the time I was focused on selling entirely into the European financial services sector and had engaged in a competitive bid with one of the UK's largest retail banks. Let's just call them National Bank for the purposes of this story.

National Bank had hundreds of branches across the UK and had almost 20 call centers spread across the country as a result of mergers and acquisitions it had made over the years. They were headquartered in Milton Keynes, a town about 90 minutes north of London. This also happened to be the UK head office location of our largest rival competitor – Rockwell.

I had created a team of people to work with me on the bid to secure National Bank's business and we had been working for 3-4 months when it was announced that we had been shortlisted as a potential provider.

It was clear also, based on the types of questions that were being asked during the sales process that Rockwell was also being actively considered. The Rockwell sales rep was using the same 'competitive landmine' technique I spoke about earlier so we were getting requests for functionality that we didn't have, and hadn't started to develop. Most of the requests were quite nuanced but it was clear that they were coming directly from Rockwell because of the specific nature of the questions.

As you might expect we were also laying our own competitive landmines for Rockwell, effectively trading blow for blow. It was clear that not a lot of functionality separated both companies and the team at National Bank were having difficulty determining what company they wished to go with.

It became clear to me that trading functional shots at each other was not going to help the situation so I scheduled a 'roadmap' day with the client. I argued that if we were going to work together for the next 5-10 years then we should be sharing our views on where we believed the market was going.

I suggested this because the company I worked for was a specialist in the space and had given a lot of thought to the future possibilities for the market. We had pretty forward-looking demonstrations, mock-ups and videos that spoke about video call centers, virtual assistants and advanced voice recognition technologies that were in their infancy at the time.

I knew the person leading the National Bank evaluation process would find what we had to say interesting for two primary reasons. Firstly, he was a geek who loved new and emerging technologies and secondly, and more importantly, he was politically astute and was on the management fast-track at National Bank so anything that made him look good, would be well received.

On the flip side, because he was politically astute, he wasn't about to hitch his wagon to a company that might not deliver the progressive solution that he wanted so we needed to ensure that we addressed any doubts he may have had in this area.

The day arrived to meet with the team from National Bank. I had carefully set up the entire day to walk the team through what it would be like to work with my company, both today and into the future.

Starting with a welcome from our CEO who had flown in from the US, we heard about the provenance of the business and how it had grown over the last 20 years to become a global player in the highly specialized world of 'mission-critical' call centers.

That was followed by a session with the UK Managing Director, who shared her stories of the past 15 years we had spent in the UK supporting some of the largest call centers that UK had. In between, we played a video that was effectively an amalgam of all of the TV ads that our customers had, set to an uplifting backing track.

All the while, we were building a picture of our company with our prospect, setting the scene for what we could do for them today, but providing context on what qualified us to get to that point.

We followed the initial presentations with a summary of the solution we were proposing, followed by a summary of our proposed project plan.

This was delivered by our head of consulting, the person whose team would deliver the solution if we were chosen. This built confidence that we had a well-proven process for deploying even the most complex networks of call centers.

We then toured our support center, demonstrating how we supported not just our products, but proactively provided help and support to call center managers, supervisors and team leaders on a daily basis.

Having seen our capabilities as they stood at that time, we then moved into looking at the future, or what we referred to as our roadmap. For this, we had presentations from our head of product development followed by product concept demonstrations from our senior product managers looking at the future of multi-media call centers, natural language voice recognition and 'assisted selling' or 'virtual assistant' technology that was in the early stages of development at that time.

Before we ended the day, I facilitated a question and answer session, firstly with our team and subsequently, with two existing customers who agreed to act as advocates for us. They were happy to answer any questions National Bank had about what it was like to be a customer of ours. The team from National Bank loved it, and although it was an exhausting day, it was clear that we had created significant distance between Rockwell and ourselves. We reinforced at every point we could during the day that 'this is all we do'. It was a deliberate ploy on my part to differentiate ourselves from Rockwell who had such diverse interests, with the call center component of their business easily one of their smallest divisions.

A few weeks later, I was on week long break in the highlands of Scotland when I received a call from the executive at National Bank. I had asked him to call me if they had come to a decision while I was away. He told me they had decided and was happy to inform me that we had been chosen.

We had in his words clearly demonstrated what made us different. It was the people and the passion we had for the industry we worked in.

No amount of product differentiation was going to do that. We managed to win a multi-million-dollar contract with National Bank because we understood what was important to the client and we prioritized in his mind that 'this is all we do'. It was like a political campaign slogan, and in many respects it shared a lot in common with running a successful campaign in the political arena. View your prospect as the electorate. Understand what is important to them. Highlight these issues as part of your campaign and ensure that they are prioritized as important by those who can vote for you.

I had a lot of respect for Rockwell and how they managed their campaign but we managed to establish what was different about us and ensure that National Bank shared our view on the importance of domain focus.

I have always made it a priority of mine to understand the competitive landscape completely. Knowing what messaging they lead with, what customers they have, how they sell, direct or indirect, who their executives are, where they have come from, all provides insight into how they are likely to compete with you. You have often heard it said, keep your friends close and your enemies even closer. This is true irrespective to what you are selling. If you do not know what or who you are competing against, you are at a major disadvantage.

Bottom line: Competition is like Darwinian theory accelerated. Adapt, overcome and grow, or die. If you are not thinking like this, you may be dead already and not even know it.

Chapter 12: Presenting and the art of storytelling.

From the time that Neanderthal man etched crude markings on the walls of his cave, through to the interactive iPad-based stories that our kids enjoy today, man has enjoyed telling and listening to stories.

Award winning journalists have always used powerful story-telling techniques to help illustrate their points in a manner that everyone can relate to. There is a reason that the US alone spends northwards of $14Bn a year on books. We love stories.

The personal and engaging nature of storytelling is a tool that the very best salespeople use. You may be skeptical of this if you are selling a product which you perceive as boring, or perhaps limiting in its storytelling application. I beg to differ. I have yet to encounter a product that you cannot tell a story about.

Does your product have customers? Tell their story. How are they using it? What value are they seeing? Has the value they've seen led to improvements in how they work, or how they meet their customer's needs? Sharing this with prospective clients is a great way to engage them. People instinctively like to be associated with success, so sharing the success of others, subliminally, suggests that by using your product or service, the prospective client will, by extension, enjoy similar success.

Let me give you an example. When I was younger, amongst other things, I wanted to become a film director. I was obsessed with movies and the way in which you could be taken from everyday reality into a word that seemed limitless. From historical settings of war to futuristic movies set in space, I loved them all.

As a teenager I wrote short stories that I dreamed of one day turning into movies of my own. There were westerns and Elizabethan adventures and portals that allowed my characters to time travel.

When I was old enough I bought a camcorder and began to shoot mini-episodes but with limited technology came pretty limited results.

Today – I use a Go-Pro and Final-cut Pro from Apple to create family montages and other fun projects, so although I haven't quite graduated to Spielberg classics, I have, thanks to Go-Pro and Apple managed to make quite a bit of progress of realizing my visual ideas.

The short movies I create are for a limited audience but give me great pleasure whenever I watch them and even more when I share them with friends and family. In fact, that's one of the other great benefits of the creation of Go-Pro, the community of people who share their videos. From skiing down mountains to proximity flying, aerial views of tropical rainforests and underwater exploration of the world's oceans. Thanks to Go-Pro you can enjoy a first person view of some of the most thrilling experiences on the planet. When you think about it, Go-Pro don't really sell cameras, they sell a lifestyle, they sell shared-experiences, they sell community, and for the next generation of movie-makers, they sell the possibility of dreams realized.

You see what Go-Pro did there? Take a humble camera and tell a story, and you can connect with a person on a level that you just can't if you take the features of the product.

This illustrates a point that is worth noting about great companies, and if you are trying to create one, take note. Stories sell.

As humans, we are social animals and we have base human instincts that must be considered when seeking to connect with other people – other humans. Firstly, to really connect with someone, a human story is powerful. It's powerful for a number or reasons, however, at its core, if it's human in nature, it's engaging, it can be related to 'emotionally' and connections and trust can be built as a result. You don't get this with PowerPoint and product features.

What's also interesting about storytelling is that the effects of it can linger for some time after the fact, and research has shown that the positive effects of storytelling can encourage desired action subliminally – this explains why we may feel more encouraged to work out after watching Rocky, or more commonly, encouraged to buy a pizza at 7pm on Saturday evening when Dominos runs an ad with panning shots of breads, dips, pizzas and soda's being poured liberally into glasses full of ice. It's 30 seconds of storytelling, perfectly timed to catch you at your weakest.

Now I'm not suggesting that you need to wait until just the right time to tell your story, but often when presented with a prospective customer, they have a real need. They need to know that you understand their need and by connecting with them through storytelling, you can not only demonstrate that you understand and can help, but you can encourage them to take that next step also.

Let's look at that concept in a little more detail.

When I first started working in sales there was a mantra that said when presenting your product or service you needed to focus on 'Benefits – not the features' . What this means in practice is this.

The features of a toothbrush may be that it comes in a range of colors and an ergonomically designed handle and bi-directional bristles. These are all features. To sell you must talk about benefits. So the benefits of the toothbrush are that it leaves your breath smelling fresh and helps you achieve a bright friendly smile.

While I definitely subscribe to the thinking that benefits are far more appropriate way to sell, contextualizing these benefits in a story that the buyer can relate to is even more powerful.

As I prepared for this chapter I took a look at the basic structure of a short story.

One good model for story structure is Algis Budrys' seven-point story structure. In summary it has:

- A character
- In a situation
- With a problem
- Who tries repeatedly to solve his problem
- But repeatedly fails (usually making the problem worse)
- Then, at the climax of the story, makes a final attempt (which might either succeed or fail, depending on the kind of story it is), after which
- The result is validated in a way that makes it clear that what we saw was in fact, the final result.

This is a structure that we can relate to from movies through to novels we've read.

If you apply this structure to your 'storytelling' you'll be surprised how effective it can be.

Here's an example.

Years ago, I had the pleasure of working with a guy called Tobias. Tobias was a very successful executive who had grown his company quickly and aggressively over a few short years. He had grown his business through acquisition as well as organic growth and at the time we met, had about 300 people working for him.

It was a software company and had a really great product for its time. Right around the time I met him, the software market was going through a change with subscription software becoming more popular.

Put simply, the software that Tobias used to sell for $2,500 per license, was now available for $50 per month on a subscription model. He was worried. He shared with me that he was concerned for the future of the business and the 300 employees and their families who relied on him making the right decisions when it came to moving the company forward.

He had tried reducing his price to compete with companies with the new subscription model but that failed as he was still many times more expensive. He also tried buying a company whose technology was already 'cloud enabled', meaning it could be accessed via the web and 'subscribed to' but that deal fell through when the company was bought by a third party.

The company I was working for sold products and services that allowed Tobias to take his existing software and sell it on a subscription basis within 8 weeks and that's exactly what we did. Using the solution I provided, Tobias was able to successfully compete with his newer rivals and because he had been around for a great deal longer than his competitors he grew that company to over 900 employees before it was sold to Microsoft for $250m less than 18 months ago.

That's a pretty powerful example that anyone in a similar situation to Tobias couldn't ignore. To make our point we've used the 7-point structure:

- A character (Tobias)
- In a situation (His business being challenged)
- With a problem (Market was changing rapidly)
- Who tries repeatedly to solve his problem (Move his software to the cloud)
- But repeatedly fails (usually making the problem worse)
- Then, at the climax of the story, makes a final attempt (which might either succeed or fail, depending on the kind of story it is), after which
- The result is validated in a way that makes it clear that what we saw was in fact, the final result (selling his company to Microsoft)

So, here's my point. Think about what stories you have, or your clients may have. This will help to validate the reasons why customers bought your product. This will resonate with prospective customers in a way that just talking about the benefits, will not.

Chapter 13: Demonstrating your product or service

If you sell a product or service that can be physically demonstrated, you no doubt receive requests from prospective customers to see your product or service in action. You might feel this is a standard enough request and one that you should respond to with a simple 'yes'. If you do, you are missing a couple of tricks that will help you engage your client more successfully and increase your sales conversion rate substantially.

It is worth looking at the request for a demonstration and determining what this request is telling you. Firstly, the request for a demo is an initial signal of intent. It means that I am interested in what you have said to the extent that I would now like some proof. It is, without further investigation, nothing more than that until you qualify a number of key points. Firstly, what would your prospective customer like to see? What interests them about your product or service?. Think about the demonstration as an opportunity for you to demonstrate not just the product, but the value that the customer will enjoy if they invest in your product. Let me give you an example.

I mentioned before my time working for Aspect, in the call center equipment market. They sold software and hardware for high-end call centers that handled thousands of calls every hour. Our customers were banks, airlines, technology companies, government services, etc. Aspect had a great product but what it didn't have was a product that you could easily demonstrate without a degree of creativity. It was, essentially a call-management platform with some reporting software so you could manage service levels in your center but that was it.

I was engaged at the time in a sales opportunity for a very large banking client with 15+ contact centers for whom they were replacing their existing solution.

I had spent a long period of time sitting with the contact center managers understanding the challenges they had. I sat with the supervisors who had inadequate reports to manage their teams, and heard them talk about the inefficiency of how calls were routed, with some centers being hugely busy while other centers had capacity. I sat with the technology team that found the software they were working with inflexible and inappropriate to meet the demands of their internal clients. This equipped me with all I needed for the demonstration.

As we prepared for the demo day, I asked the client if they could invite some representatives from the call center, some supervisors, one or two of the center managers, as well as the technical evaluation committee and the executive sponsor. I argued that it would be useful to ensure that if they were going to be asked to use the solution that was bought that they should at least be given the opportunity to give some feedback on it. The client agreed.

On the day of the demonstration we had our presentation space split into 3, representing 3 different call centers. We simulated calls coming into each center, with calls automatically flowing to the first available agent across the centers, making sure one site wasn't overwhelmed.

We showed the supervisor screens updating in real time so service levels could be monitored, and we showed the financial impact of this in a real-time staffing display.

Throughout the demonstration I spoke to each of the stakeholders about the challenges that I had observed when we were on-site with them.

I showed how working with Aspect would allow them to overcome these challenges and I showed the commercial savings to be had by doing so, to the executives with commercial responsibility.

The response was universally positive. We had demonstrated that we understood the challenges as well as the commercial sensitivities of any decision they might make. We also demonstrated that we had listened and were capable of delivering solutions that spoke directly to the challenges they faced.

The fact that we had demonstrated the product was almost secondary. It was important for sure, but more important was the demonstration of understanding that we had.

We secured their business. It was a 7 figure deal that has delivered millions in revenue for Aspect and still does today, almost 20 years on. That was one powerful demo in retrospect.

Just think about how you demonstrate your product or service. Most companies have a standard demo, or a scripted demo that they feel meets the requirements of most and salespeople are often blindly led through sales training with the demo forming a small part of that training. The demo is hugely important. It is your opportunity to have your prospective customer spend time feeling what it would be like to be a customer, to use your product or service.

The demo is a chance for you to tell a story, with your customer as the central figure. Much like the stories I read my two children, when you put them at the center of the story, they are even more invested, more excited. We may be selling to adults but it's human nature for that person to project themselves and their experiences on your product and if that 'projection' isn't positive, you may just lose that prospect.

We have all experienced pushy salespeople who clearly don't understand what we need, or have made ill-informed assumptions about who we are and what we need.

Just like any relationship in life you can only truly get to know that person by listening when they talk and being genuinely interested in what they are saying, with a good measure of questioning thrown in.

Investing the time to do this will give you returns when it comes time to demonstrate your product or service. You will be able to quote the challenges they shared with you. This will build confidence. You will be able to relate their challenges to how your product or service will address them. This too builds confidence and finally, you will be able to personalize the story such that they can relate intimately to what it will be like to be a customer of yours.

When you have achieved this, you are a long way down the path to this company becoming a customer.

Bottom Line: A demonstration of your product should demonstrate you understand your customer, their challenges and how you will address them. It is not a product demonstration – it's a 'I listened to you and I can help you' demonstration.

Chapter 14: Reference selling

Some of the most powerful supporters I've had throughout my sales career have been my base of customers, past and present. I believe people buy from people and when a customer buys from me, they are trusting me that I will look after their needs, I will deliver what I committed to (on behalf of my company) and I will help them realize the benefits we spoke of during the sales cycle.

This may sound like an obvious statement but it is an unfortunately regular occurrence that this does not happen. For various reasons, salespeople move on from one deal to the next, seeking to maximize their commission and leaving the customer who just bought their product or service in the hands of their colleagues. This is not that unusual, and there are some that would argue that the type of salesperson who 'hunts' new business is not the same as the 'farmer' who helps that customer to grow as an existing client. I subscribe to that theory to an extent; however as a salesperson, I have always sought to remain engaged with clients after the sale has closed. It helped to make sure that what I committed to was being delivered, but also to maintain the relationship and respect that I have earned from that customer.

As my sales career grew, I started to appreciate one of the major benefits of this approach, namely the ability to bring these clients into new sales engagements to provide references for me.

References from existing clients are very important for a number of reasons. Firstly, they are independent assessments of me, my company and my product or service. This is someone other than you as the salesperson (whose job it is to espouse the virtues of your offering) sharing their experiences with your prospective customer.

This is far more powerful than anything you could say as the prospect is essentially saying 'I had the same challenges as you had and we worked with Ferdi's company to solve the issues – and we are very happy with the results'. Pretty powerful, I think you'd agree.

The second benefit of reference selling is that it's a major milestone in your sales process if you manage to get your prospective customer to commit their time to taking a day out to meet with an existing customer to discuss their experience.

If your prospect was not seriously considering your proposal they wouldn't take the time to do this, so you should view participation as an indication of intent, i.e. It should be viewed in the context of other positive signs as to how your sales process is progressing.

The third benefit of reference selling is that it pays a compliment to both parties. It compliments your existing customer by asking them to share their successful story with another company. Subliminally, you are saying to that customer that you respect them and feel like they made a great decision and executed well on that decision. So much so that you believe other companies who faced similar problems will want to hear how they did it.

That's a pretty nice compliment. For your prospect, you are showing them how important they are to you that you are facilitating a reference for them. On a related note, I have always tried to ensure that the reference took place on-site with the company providing the reference. This adds further weight to the reference call as it takes your prospect out of their environment and allows them to become a 'guest' of the company that is providing the reference. These are all small things but collectively they make a real difference to your prospect.

Preparation:
As with all things related to your sales cycle the degree to which you benefit from a reference visit will be directly proportional to the preparation you put into it.

Here are number of tasks you should complete before any reference visit.

- Make sure you fully understand the pain-points of your customer. These are the issues that you uncovered during your discovery process. The important point to note here is that these 'pain points' cannot simply be the issues that you identified. They must be identified by your prospect as being a pain point for them.

- Identify an existing client who most closely matches the circumstances that your prospective client is faced with. The closer the challenges faced by your prospect are to the challenges overcome by your customer the greater the benefit of the reference visit to your prospect.

- Discuss what's important for your prospect to get from the reference visit so that you are prepared and have prioritized what the key take-aways are from the reference visit.

- Brief the company that is providing the reference visit to ensure that they are aware of what is important to your prospect.

- Prepare an agenda for the visit and time-bound each section to ensure that all of the key points are covered in the limited time that you have.

- Offer to drive your prospect to the reference site. I personally made a habit of firstly inviting the prospect to my office for a pre-visit briefing where I would share the 'evaluation' journey that my customer had been on before choosing my company. This allows you to set some key competitive landmines, advise them that my customer sat where they are and had choices, but ultimately decided to work with us for reasons a, b and c.

Once completed, I would then drive them to the reference site. This gives you valuable time in a more relaxed setting with your prospect to discuss their thoughts on the process to date, what steps they have yet to take before making a decision etc. Take every opportunity you can to get this kind of time with your prospect.

When you are at the site, your job is simply to facilitate, keep the agenda moving so the key points are made and to generally remain quiet while your existing customer explains why your company was the right choice for them. This is not the time for additional selling. For the reference visit to be most beneficial it needs to be a conversation among peers rather than a conversation peppered with the salesperson interrupting or adding positive comments to the visit.

Once the visit is over take the time to debrief from the session with your prospect. Were there any points left unanswered? (if you did your job correctly there won't be), do they have any concerns after the visit? (again, these should be minimal if you prepared well). The purpose of the debrief should be to get to a shortlist of issues prior to closing. The more you prepared for the reference visit, the shorter this list will be.

Finally, make sure you thank your customer. It's a commitment to take time out of their day to support a reference visit. You should make sure that their generosity is repaid, whether that's tickets to a game, a nice meal or a bottle of their favorite wine.

If you follow the steps outlined, you will have a successful reference visit and substantially increase your chances of securing that deal.

Chapter 15: Negotiation – Getting to win-win

When the average person thinks about negotiation, it's typically informed by what they've seen on TV, or witnessed in market-stall type negotiations. It involves a back and forth on price with the two parties typically agreeing on a compromise number with the stereo-typical 'let's meet in the middle' being the final words spoken before a handshake to conclude the deal.

It's true that commoditized lower value deals can result in this type of 'negotiation'; however, if you are interested in negotiating larger deals and improving your closure rate, then you should make one very important shift in your thinking, and it's this. Negotiation starts on the first engagement you have with your prospective customer and ends (for that deal, at least) on the day you have a signed contract. Every step in between involves negotiation of some kind, and for the skilled negotiator results in the final deal closure being a matter of relative ease.

Let me explain what I mean. When you first engage with a prospective customer (via phone, for example), you are working with one of the most valuable currencies available – time. That currency is limited on our part and limited on the part of the person you are calling, yet you are choosing to 'spend' that currency picking up the phone to speak to them.

You are doing this because you have something of value to impart to the person you are calling. If you don't truly believe this to be the case, you need to work on understanding your value proposition before you pick up the phone, or admit to yourself that if you were in their shoes, you wouldn't take the call. If the latter is true, you are either selling the wrong product, or targeting the wrong person.

If you accept that 'time' is the currency we are trading in sales as a premise, then understanding the concept that we are in a state of 'constant negotiation' during the sales process should be easy.

Negotiation is not just the penultimate stage of your sales process - it is part of the fabric of your entire sales process.

We are negotiating when a prospective customer picks up the phone and says 'hello' and you have 10 seconds to convince them that what you have to trade, in return for their currency (time) is valuable enough for them to want to listen further to you.

If you succeed in this negotiation, you then move to negotiating your desired outcome, which may be to meet face to face, or for your prospect to commit to allocating time to sit in on a webinar.

When you meet with them, you are negotiating to get them to commit to a detailed 'discovery phase' so you can determine exactly how your company can help them. This continues right up the point where you secure their business and they sign a contract. I refer to this as the process of 'continuous negotiation' for obvious reasons.

There a few major points to note about a process of continuous negotiation. The first is that by being conscious of the fact that negotiation is continuous you don't fall into the trap that so many salespeople make which is to concede something for nothing. This is not always apparent. For example, a prospect may observe that they found your presentation of interest and ask you to send it to them so they can distribute to a broader team.

You could view this as a positive, and it is, but blindly sending them a copy of your carefully crafted presentation as opposed to asking who they would like to send it to, and agreeing to present to that broader audience personally demands some negotiation. The prospect is still getting what they want, but you are getting face time with a group of potential influencers that you might not otherwise have had, if you chose not to negotiate that. This is a simplistic example but it's easily missed.

In the same way that you must be attuned to opportunity for sales, you must be attuned to potential negotiation opportunities also. When you are attuned, these opportunities don't pass you by, you recognize them as they present themselves, or you create an opportunity for the negotiation to occur.

As a related side note, you can create opportunities for negotiation by creating items of value for your customer, e.g. a presentation, a study, a return on investment template etc. These are tradable for other commitments from your customer. For example, if you have created a spreadsheet with variables that once completed helps calculate the Return On Investment (ROI) that they will achieve by deploying your solution, that's of real value. Don't give it away without getting something in return.

This brings us to the second major point. I believe consciously and continuously negotiating at each stage in the sales process makes it easier, and more likely to get a deal done at the end. Think of it this way. If you negotiate at each stage and are successful in those negotiations, the chances are that you are more likely to win as you are testing the commitment of the prospect at each stage.

If, for example, you try to negotiate a presentation to the senior executive team and your contact, who is a member of that team, says no, there is either an issue that your contact hasn't shared, or they don't feel you have significant enough value to bring to that meeting.

If you feel you have value to bring, for example, by introducing your CEO at the meeting to talk about the company roadmap, and they still say no, you need to treat that push-back as a potential sign of weakness in your value proposition.

There may be many valid reasons why they don't want it to happen, but in my experience push-back as part of these negotiations should be a cause for concern. If you were selling against me, I wouldn't accept no. I would create enough value for it to make sense and you would be at an immediate disadvantage.

My point here is that the continuous negotiation allows you to sense-check and qualify your deal. Each successful negotiation in the process is a green light for you to proceed to the next stage until finally, you are discussing contract terms and putting ink on paper.

The basics of negotiation:

Entire books have been written on the subject of negotiation and the plethora of negotiation strategies and tactics that exist; however, in this chapter I wanted to share with you what I've personally learned when it comes to negotiation

To become a skilled negotiator takes practice but let's start with the basics, which, when used consistently, will help you negotiate more effectively, protect your price-point and create other opportunities for further sales in the future.

Here are my top 10 lessons for more effective negotiation.

Lesson number 1: Put yourself in the shoes of the buyer

Everyone likes to feel like they are understood. In a business negotiation, the buyer wants you to have an appreciation for what their needs are and what they are willing to pay to have those needs met. Separate to your understanding of the dollars and cents discussion is a more fundamental issue – empathy. Empathy essentially means having an appreciation for the circumstances of another person and reacting positively to that. In the context of negotiation, empathy doesn't mean dropping the price just because a buyer doesn't want to pay it. It means creating options for that person that reasonably helps them achieve what is truly important to them, while not compromising the things that are truly important to you.

By taking the time to fully appreciate and understand what is most important to the buyer, you can navigate the negotiation more effectively. There may be 10 'asks' during the negotiation. 5 may be must-haves, and 5 nice-to-haves. The challenge that you must rise to is understanding which bucket each of the asks falls into so you can help the buyer achieve the must-haves while diplomatically leveraging out the nice-to-have's. I've found that you can gain insights into most of the must-haves before the final stages of the negotiation.

Lesson number 2: Strive for win-win

Another common misconception regarding negotiation is that in order for you to win – the other party must lose. This is not the case. Negotiation involves compromise, and it should always result in a mutually beneficial outcome – a win-win situation for both you and your customer.

This is not always easy to achieve but it's something that you should strive for, not just to successfully negotiate on the occasion in question, but to ensure that your customer is happy to negotiate with you in the future.

If you successfully get what you want from a negotiation, but the other party feels like they got a raw deal, that may be the last negotiation you have with them.

Lesson number 3: Create options for greater flexibility

When you are negotiating, having a number of potential options helps you avoid 'painting yourself into a corner'. If you think of a negotiation process as getting from point A to point B across a map, then options represent your ability to overcome obstacles that may sit between you and your destination.

For example; if you are trying to protect your price point in a negotiation, and your customer feels like they need more, reducing your price is not an option but perhaps extending the terms of your support, or offering additional training, or providing more favorable payment terms are options that allow you to overcome that objection and move closer to your desired outcome. Think about what options you can provide that are of value, so the customer feels better about the deal, but you can protect what's important to you.

Lesson number 4: Know your 'asks' before closing

This may sound obvious, but it takes some forethought to really think about what's important to you before you enter negotiations.

What is your desired outcome? Is there a number at which it doesn't make sense for you to do a deal? What priority do you give to each 'ask' that you have?

If you got 3 out of the 5 'asks' would you be happy?

The reason it's important to know what you want from the negotiation, is that it allows you to understand what you are prepared to trade, in return for protecting what is really important to you. Compromise goes hand in hand with negotiation and knowing what you are willing to compromise on is step 1 towards achieving the win-win I spoke of earlier.

Lesson number 5: Park the difficult items and maintain momentum
In every negotiation there exists the potential for contention. Difficult conversations can arise and in some cases stop the negotiations in their tracks. To avoid this, if you feel that you are at an impasse, ask that you note the issue as something that is still to be agreed and move on.

This achieves two things. It allows you to keep the momentum of the negotiation going, while also narrowing down the issues to a final list. You will both have a final list and conclusion to the negotiation will arrive as you trade off the remaining issues with each other.

Lesson number 6: Know the impact of each concession
This sounds obvious but it's surprising how often rookie negotiators concede on a point without fully appreciating the impact of that concession. For example, if a customer asks that support hours be increased by a number of hours it may seem like a small concession to increase the hours from 5pm to 7pm, but this can cause significant operational challenges and of course increased cost. In support organizations, to provide two additional hours of cover can require additional headcount, employment contract amendments, back-up coverage, etc.

Knowing what the impact of each concession may be is crucial to your ability to intelligently negotiate. You may win the deal, but end up losing out financially because of a concession you made, ignorant of the consequences.

Lesson number 7: Keep it positive

Negotiations can be challenging and occasionally nerves and tempers may be tested but to successfully negotiate you must maintain composure and keep the tone of the negotiations positive at all times.

Even when faced with challenging push-back, you can keep it positive by acknowledging the other person's perspective. For example, you might say 'I can tell that's important to you, and I'm bearing that in mind as I think about how we can resolve this issue'.

Acknowledgement is key as it shows the customer that you empathize with their position or circumstance, but it is not a concession. You may choose to park that issue for your final list, meaning you can negotiate the bulk of what you want before finally dealing with the challenging issues. With a few items remaining, typically both parties will want to conclude the discussion, and this is far more likely to end positively, if you've managed to keep the tone positive throughout your discussions.

Lesson number 8: Protect your price

Protecting your price in a negotiation is not about taking a stance on the cost per unit, or overall deal value, it's about preparing yourself with options that can be traded against a request to lower your price. As an example, rather than lowering your price you can extend the term of the agreement, or allow the customer to pay in instalments. There may be very little cost to you to do this but have a lot of value for your customer.

Lesson number 9: Give more get more

A common request from a prospective customer during negotiations is to ask for more.

More discount, more options, more time to pay their invoice, etc. These requests are not always negative. For example, if a customer asks for a bigger discount, are they prepared to order more from you? If they ask for more time to pay, are they prepared to commit to a 2-year contract as opposed to a 1-year contract. You get my point. Negotiation is intended to be a win for both parties so be open to requests to 'give' to your customer as this is very often an opportunity for you to 'get' more in return.

Lesson number 10: Close, close, close.
In negotiations, you should always be striving to move towards closing. This may seem obvious but I've seen negotiations drag on for weeks longer than they need to because both parties were in engaged in constant negotiation rather than closing. Closing in a negotiation is often about being crystal clear with the other party about what closure looks like. For example, saying to the customer 'If we can resolve issues A to F then are we agreed that we are in a position to sign contracts?' Clearly this is a pretty frontal way of stating it, but when you are negotiating, clarity is your friend and should be introduced early and often.

Statements like this keep closure on top of the agenda. If it isn't, you will continue to negotiate and risk the possibility of your customer introducing new points of negotiation, further elongating discussions and potentially risking the deal.

In summary, a large part of success in negotiation comes from being prepared, knowing what you want, being open to compromise, but being intelligent about how this compromise is arrived at.

Chapter 16: Closing the sale

One of the great clichés of sales is ABC – **A**lways **B**e **C**losing. It's a cliché for a reason, but like many clichés it is often disregarded. Do so at your peril. The reality is this. From the very first interaction with a prospective customer you are either moving towards closing the sale or moving away from it.

I have always viewed closing as a series of small steps that ultimately ends in receipt of a signed contract. To get to this point I've found it useful for your prospect to get used to agreeing to various requests from you. Not all requests need to be large – it can be a request for a call, or a request for a meeting, or to attend an event, or even a quick business lunch.

At some point in the future you are going to ask them for their business, so, simplistically, they should get used to hearing requests from you as early as possible and as often as practical during the sales cycle. To be clear, I don't advocate being a pest with your prospect, but you should be continually testing their engagement levels as your progress through the sales process. Equally, if they ask for something from you, always, and I mean ALWAYS ask for something in return. If they ask you for a presentation, ask them to invite anyone else who may be involved in the decision making process. If they ask you for pricing, ask them for a meeting to discuss the requirements in detail so you can make the pricing as accurate as possible. If they ask for a discount, ask them for a larger order or a longer contract term. You get the idea.

The more they get used to you asking them for things in return for requests that they make, the easier it will be to close the sale when, at the end of the sales cycle, you recount all you have done for them to get to this point, and it will not come as a surprise to them that you are now asking for their custom in return.

I wrote earlier of the importance of having a well-defined sales process, the end point of which (provided it is well managed) will naturally be agreement and signature of a contract or agreement to proceed.

If you explain this process early to a prospective client, and keep them apprised of where they are in that process, you are also creating an environment for the 'close' to happen naturally, at the allotted time. This doesn't mean you say to a client that 'Now – we are moving into the closing phase of my sales cycle', it simply means that you remind them of what steps you have completed and what steps are left before you ask them for their business.

Your conversation may go something like this. "So Steve, as I outlined originally we took a look at your challenges using our health check tool. We reviewed the report that came from that and presented our findings to the executive team. As you know, we just need to agree the final scope of work that you think you'd like to address at this point before we can issue a proposal, and my understanding is, at the point you receive that, you simply need to review at your weekly management meeting and subject to agreement there, your CEO can then sign off on our proposal before we move to contract – is my understanding correct?" This is your way of reminding your prospect that you have a formal process to equip them with the information they need to make a decision, and that you understand the process they need to go through to make that decision. I made it my business to ensure that I constantly checked this process with my prospects.

You will find that this may change, and prompting your prospect brings that to light. For example, Steve may respond – 'that's correct, but our CEO can only recommend it. Agreement actually comes after the board has reviewed it and they sit every two months'.

That kind of puts a different complexion on things and could significantly affect how you are reporting and forecasting this deal within your company.

Make a habit of replaying the process to your prospect and you will have fewer surprises and a lot more predictability in your sales forecast.

As we discussed during the 'sales process' section of this book, the process makes it easier for your prospect to understand how they buy your product, but more importantly, it gives you a process through which you can move your pipeline of prospective customers. You will lose some along the way, naturally, but in time, if you have a consistent methodology for selling, you will be able to predict with more accuracy what percentage of that business you are likely to close, and become more adept at doing so.

Time is the enemy

One of the most challenging issues in closing is the procrastination or inaction of others, and nowhere is this potentially more challenging than when you are engaged in concluding an important deal.

In all my years of selling, I've rarely seen a deal get better the longer it gets delayed, but I've seen a great number of deals get killed or reduced in scope as a result of delays, as people's roles change, competing projects take priority, or any number of alternate changes take place in the prospects organization. Time – truly is the enemy of sales.

We've all been there. It's coming up to end of quarter and that deal you need to make your numbers is progressing at a pedestrian pace. It's challenging – but this can be avoided.

There are a number of key activities you should undertake to ensure you don't end up with that end-of-quarter crunch.

1. **Have a sales process**. If you can get your prospective customer to commit to your sales process rather than their buying process, you can create some predictability in your forecast. Your sales process will include actions and timelines that you can control and should support closure in timeframes that are optimized for your business.

2. **Seek continuous commitment**. This is a theme that we've covered a number of times in this book. Don't leave it until the final weeks of a sales process to ask your prospect for commitments. By asking for a series of commitments throughout the sales process, when you ask for their business there's no surprise e.g. ask for little commitments at each stage in your sales process, i.e. commit to a discovery session, commit to a custom demo, commit to a meeting with the sponsor, commit to a reference call with another client of yours etc. Seeking continuous commitment is not only a great qualifier as you progress through your process, it also sets the expectation with your prospective customer that you ARE going to ask for commitments in return for things you do for them, and as such when you ask for the order within a given timeframe (e.g. by end of quarter) your chances of securing that commitment are significantly improved as you've already established and tested commitment throughout your sales process/engagement with the prospect.

3. **Have a clear close plan**. A close plan is part of your overall sales process and will include a detailed, step by step timeline and action plan to close your deal. If you don't have one – you have zero predictability. This is for your benefit, but it is worthless unless your buyer agrees to it.

Once you've created your close plan, discuss the timing and activities for each stage in the plan with your prospective customer. They will either agree with it, or tell you what is, or isn't possible. The worst that will happen is you get greater visibility of the steps to closure. Another clear benefit of this approach is that if a prospective buyer starts to deviate from the close plan, you can remind them of the fact that you both reviewed and mutually agreed the steps to closure. It doesn't guarantee that they will stick to the close plan but a plan that you have both reviewed and agreed means you can re-calibrate the plan jointly should dates start to slip or activities fail to be completed.

Bottom line: Closing the sale starts on day one. As soon as you engage a prospective customer you are either moving towards or moving away from that close date. The very best salespeople set the stage for closing right from the get-go. If you are not closing, you are not selling. Period.

Chapter 17: The 10 key habits of great salespeople

As we approach the end of this book I wanted to take a little time to cover what I believe are the 10 key things that you must do to be successful in sales. The list is not intended to be exhaustive, but rather, it is intended to be the 10 things that I deem to be most important when I look at what helped me achieve success in sales.

1.Pick up the phone

This might seem like an obvious part of a salesperson's job but in recent years it's become increasingly challenging to get the attention of buyers, as they are bombarded with requests for their time. I've found the phone to be the single most effective means of getting their attention. Nothing beats a one to one conversation and no other medium provides that immediate feedback loop that comes from a call, with the exception of face to face.

It appears to me that as it's become more challenging with voicemail and call screening that a lot of salespeople view the phone with skepticism, or that they view a 'cold call' as beneath them. As with every stage in your sales process, the success of the calls will be directly proportional to the preparation you put in, in advance of the call.

If you are informed, and have real value to bring to the person you are calling, it's your responsibility to keep trying until you get to speak with them. Get used to picking up the phone and watch your results increase – dramatically.

2. Do what you say you are going to do

This is a simple one, yet as a buyer in my own company, I've seen this abused many times by salespeople who commit to coming back to me with a proposal by Wednesday, only to deliver it on Thursday or Friday.

When we met, they committed to sending me a case study for a similar customer and yet when their proposal arrives, the case study is missing. On the face of it, this may seem small, or a genuine omission. I view it differently. If you say you are going to do something, do it. It demonstrates that you are a person of your word. It demonstrates that you can be trusted. If I get your proposal exactly when you said I would, it builds confidence. If I receive the case study, it shows that you have good attention to detail and care about the experience I have as a customer. In essence, I am consciously, or subconsciously thinking that this is the experience I will have as a customer and if you deliver on every commitment you made during the sales process, I can expect that to continue after the deal has closed.

Conversely, if I have had a series of missed commitments, that raises alarm bells and I am extremely unlikely to want to do business with you. I am your prospective customer. I am your means of earning an income and should be treated with the respect that this position deserves. Trust me. Delivering on every one of your commitments will earn you respect and trust, both of which are the necessary foundations for sales, and the bigger the deal the more important this becomes.

3. Strive for excellence

While watching an interview with the rapper and cultural icon Jay-Z recently, he spoke about his definition of excellence

Excellence in his world was not about 'being hot' for a year or two. It wasn't about having a hit record or a platinum album. He added that in the sports world 'It's not about getting a half-court basket once', it was about being at the top, and being able to take and sink these shots consistently, for an extended period of time. A decade or more of consistency was, in his world, excellence. And so it is in sales.

There's a saying in sales that 'you are only as good as your last deal', meaning that unless you are closing deals on a consistent basis, you are not delivering the goods. I agree with this to an extent but would reword this slightly to 'You are only as good as your next deal', meaning that it's the salesperson who is constantly working on their next deal and consistently closing that delivers excellence in their role. I mentioned a number of times in this book about the trap of roller coaster selling. The trap of closing a deal before looking for your next one. Consistency and excellence comes from putting in the work on new deals, while you are closing current ones. Remember, it's the work you do in the off-season that prepares you for prime time. Be excellent.

4. Don't believe the hype

I first started seeing success in sales in my early twenties. I was closing deals and cashing commission checks. On the face of it, I couldn't lose. My close rate was extremely high and it would have been easy to become complacent. I didn't let that happen and have been able to consistently close business over 20 years in my chosen profession. I've seen salespeople who worked hard to get to a similar position early on in their career and eventually they start to believe the hype. They believe they can't lose and before they know it, they become complacent and start to expect to win, without applying the same level of work, the same drive that they had when they were hungry for every deal.

The number or value of deals you've closed in the past have no bearing on the deal you are working on right now.

You need to work just as hard, be just as hungry and maintain the humility that you had when you started to ensure you stay on top. Be confident, by all means, but don't forget the basics. Stay humble.

5. Sell with your team

In chapter 6 of this book 'Never lose alone', I spoke about the importance of team selling. Apart from the obvious benefits of having multiple perspectives on a deal, team based selling helps to build confidence with your prospect by showing depth in the team. It also allows you to align resources with their obvious counterparts in an account, e.g. technical pre-sales working with your prospects tech team.

Equally important is the fact that you have additional 'eyes and ears' in the account to give you well-rounded insights into how your proposal is being received by representatives across the business rather than just with the person with whom you are dealing. You should not underestimate the importance of having non-sales related resources in the account as your prospect will feel more comfortable sharing their thoughts with your colleagues if they feel they are not being 'sold to'.

6. Negotiate from day 1

For many salespeople, the act of negotiation is seen as something that happens towards the end of a sales process. Nothing could be further from the truth. You should be negotiating from day one. Think of negotiation as a process, a journey that runs parallel to the sales process. You are negotiating at each and every stage. When you first speak with your prospect, you negotiate to get their time. When you meet with them, you negotiate a follow up presentation.
When you set the date for the presentation, you negotiate to have the right people in the room.

When you present, you negotiate a trial of your product or service in return for dedicated resources from your prospect.

And so it continues until the final stage of the negotiation, which is for a signed contract. If you have done your job properly, you will know the outcome of the negotiation before you sit down to discuss a single point of the contract. This is what we mean when we say negotiate – from day 1.

7. Get to no quickly – qualify, qualify, qualify

If you look at your pipeline today, how accurate do you feel it is? What percentage of deals that you are working on will move to closure? 50%? 30%? If it's 50%, then half of what you are working on is a waste of your time and resources. This is why it is important to qualify your deals and be just as focused on 'getting to no' as you are about 'getting to yes'. This may seem counter-intuitive to some salespeople who believe that everyone can be 'sold to'. This is not the case, as evidenced by your hit rate.

If 50% of people are not buying you need to focus more on qualifying out of deals that make no sense for you to be involved. In many cases that 'deal' you are working on is nothing more than tire-kicking on behalf of that 'prospect' you are working with.

The best salespeople qualify out quickly and make sure that the return on the time they are spending working on deals is maximized.

8. Sell what you believe in

The job of selling is difficult enough without adding the challenge of trying to sell something you don't believe in. It is far easier to be passionate about something you believe in and have faith in. This passion and faith is immediately obvious to a prospective customer and comes across in everything you do from the quality of your interactions to the quality of your proposals and presentations.

You can't fake this. Prospects see through it, so make sure that whatever you are selling is something you believe delivers real value. It makes your job a great deal easier and far more enjoyable.

I've seen salespeople question the value of what they are selling before a presentation, and despite their best efforts, it was obvious to the prospect that this was the case when answering questions during and after the presentation. You cannot in all good conscience 'sell' something you don't believe in. If you are selling something you don't believe in right now, do yourself a favor. Hit the job boards and look for products and services that you know are delivering something of value for its customers and go work for them. You'll be happier and more successful as a result.

9. Don't fool yourself

When you first start building your pipeline, either as a new salesperson, or in a new company, it's easy to chase anything that moves because you are not that busy. You might justify this on the basis that you have nothing better to do, so why not meet with prospect A, B or C because something 'might' come out of it. There 'may' be a deal to be had. This is a common mistake and essentially comes down to people fooling themselves and often ignoring the obvious lack of opportunity.

The internal dialogue that we have with ourselves in these circumstances is very important as it helps us justify our activity, or it helps us to critically assess our activity. Generally speaking, you need far more of the latter. You must be critical on an ongoing basis of where and how you are spending your time. What I've learned over time is that if you ask the right qualifying questions such as 'who benefits from this project?' and 'what happens if you do nothing?' (amongst other questions) and you still think what you are working on is a waste of time, you need to bite the bullet and not hope that you can turn it around.

Diplomatically, thank the prospect for their interest, and acknowledge that right now they don't appear to be ready to enter a buying process and tactfully retreat to go spend your time working on something productive.
Be ruthless about this qualification.

10. Pay it forward

If you've been fortunate enough to be successful in sales, you will rise through the ranks into sales management, head of sales, perhaps global head of sales. You have a duty to share what you've learned with your team and to support and mentor them. I've seen great salespeople move up the ranks only to discover that what makes a great salesperson doesn't necessarily make a great manager. The biggest contribution you can make is to spend time developing your team so that what made you successful can be transferred and replicated for the benefit of the individuals and the company. Success, I've learned, comes more from being able to do this than it does from micro-managing sales opportunities even when you become a manager.

Your success as a manager will be measured by how proficient you become at building your team, so remember – pay it forward.

That's as good a sentence as any to complete this chapter, and the book on. I hope you've found it useful and that wherever you are in your sales career that you'll benefit from some of the learnings covered across the chapters of this book.

Sales can be an extremely rewarding career, and for those who dedicate themselves to understanding both the art and science of sales, its benefits can be enjoyed far beyond your daily work, helping you achieve what you want in life, financially, professionally and personally.

Now, go sell something!

Printed in Great Britain
by Amazon

82389876R00082